OPPOSING VIEWPOINTS®

# TOBACCO AND SMOKING

# Other Books of Related Interest

OPPOSING VIEWPOINTS®

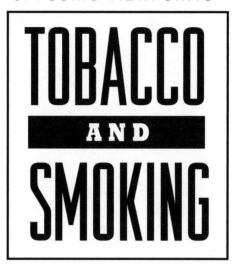

# TOBACCO AND SMOKING

Karen F. Balkin, *Book Editor*

Bruce Glassman, *Vice President*
Bonnie Szumski, *Publisher*
Helen Cothran, *Managing Editor*

OPPOSING
VIEWPOINTS®
SERIES

GREENHAVEN
PRESS®

THOMSON
★ ™
GALE

San Diego • Detroit • New York • San Francisco • Cleveland
New Haven, Conn. • Waterville, Maine • London • Munich

*For more information, contact*
Greenhaven Press
27500 Drake Rd.
Farmington Hills, MI 48331-3535
Or you can visit our Internet site at http://www.gale.com

LIBRARY OF CONGRESS CATALOGING-IN-PUBLICATION DATA

Tobacco and smoking / Karen F. Balkin, book editor.
    p. cm. — (Opposing viewpoints series)
    Includes bibliographical references and index.
    ISBN 0-7377-2248-7 (lib. : alk. paper) — ISBN 0-7377-2249-5 (pbk. : alk. paper)
    1. Tobacco habit. 2. Smoking. I. Balkin, Karen F., 1949– . II. Opposing viewpoints series (Unnumbered)
HV5733.T62  2005
362.29'6—dc22                                                2003067502

Printed in the United States of America

> "Congress shall make no law. . . abridging the freedom of speech, or of the press."

*First Amendment to the U.S. Constitution*

The basic foundation of our democracy is the First Amendment guarantee of freedom of expression. The Opposing Viewpoints Series is dedicated to the concept of this basic freedom and the idea that it is more important to practice it than to enshrine it.

# Contents

# Why Consider Opposing Viewpoints?

*"The only way in which a human being can make some approach to knowing the whole of a subject is by hearing what can be said about it by persons of every variety of opinion and studying all modes in which it can be looked at by every character of mind. No wise man ever acquired his wisdom in any mode but this."*

John Stuart Mill

In our media-intensive culture it is not difficult to find differing opinions. Thousands of newspapers and magazines and dozens of radio and television talk shows resound with differing points of view. The difficulty lies in deciding which opinion to agree with and which "experts" seem the most credible. The more inundated we become with differing opinions and claims, the more essential it is to hone critical reading and thinking skills to evaluate these ideas. Opposing Viewpoints books address this problem directly by presenting stimulating debates that can be used to enhance and teach these skills. The varied opinions contained in each book examine many different aspects of a single issue. While examining these conveniently edited opposing views, readers can develop critical thinking skills such as the ability to compare and contrast authors' credibility, facts, argumentation styles, use of persuasive techniques, and other stylistic tools. In short, the Opposing Viewpoints Series is an ideal way to attain the higher-level thinking and reading skills so essential in a culture of diverse and contradictory opinions.

In addition to providing a tool for critical thinking, Opposing Viewpoints books challenge readers to question their own strongly held opinions and assumptions. Most people form their opinions on the basis of upbringing, peer pressure, and personal, cultural, or professional bias. By reading carefully balanced opposing views, readers must directly confront new ideas as well as the opinions of those with whom they disagree. This is not to simplistically argue that everyone who reads opposing views will—or should—change his or her opinion. Instead, the series enhances readers' understanding of their own views by encouraging confrontation with opposing ideas. Careful examination of others' views can lead to the readers' understanding of the logical inconsistencies in their own opinions, perspective on why they hold an opinion, and the consideration of the possibility that their opinion requires further evaluation.

## Evaluating Other Opinions

To ensure that this type of examination occurs, Opposing Viewpoints books present all types of opinions. Prominent spokespeople on different sides of each issue as well as well-known professionals from many disciplines challenge the reader. An additional goal of the series is to provide a forum for other, less known, or even unpopular viewpoints. The opinion of an ordinary person who has had to make the decision to cut off life support from a terminally ill relative, for example, may be just as valuable and provide just as much insight as a medical ethicist's professional opinion. The editors have two additional purposes in including these less known views. One, the editors encourage readers to respect others' opinions—even when not enhanced by professional credibility. It is only by reading or listening to and objectively evaluating others' ideas that one can determine whether they are worthy of consideration. Two, the inclusion of such viewpoints encourages the important critical thinking skill of objectively evaluating an author's credentials and bias. This evaluation will illuminate an author's reasons for taking a particular stance on an issue and will aid in readers' evaluation of the author's ideas.

It is our hope that these books will give readers a deeper understanding of the issues debated and an appreciation of the complexity of even seemingly simple issues when good and honest people disagree. This awareness is particularly important in a democratic society such as ours in which people enter into public debate to determine the common good. Those with whom one disagrees should not be regarded as enemies but rather as people whose views deserve careful examination and may shed light on one's own.

Thomas Jefferson once said that "difference of opinion leads to inquiry, and inquiry to truth." Jefferson, a broadly educated man, argued that "if a nation expects to be ignorant and free . . . it expects what never was and never will be." As individuals and as a nation, it is imperative that we consider the opinions of others and examine them with skill and discernment. The Opposing Viewpoints Series is intended to help readers achieve this goal.

David L. Bender and Bruno Leone,
Founders

---

Greenhaven Press anthologies primarily consist of previously published material taken from a variety of sources, including periodicals, books, scholarly journals, newspapers, government documents, and position papers from private and public organizations. These original sources are often edited for length and to ensure their accessibility for a young adult audience. The anthology editors also change the original titles of these works in order to clearly present the main thesis of each viewpoint and to explicitly indicate the opinion presented in the viewpoint. These alterations are made in consideration of both the reading and comprehension levels of a young adult audience. Every effort is made to ensure that Greenhaven Press accurately reflects the original intent of the authors included in this anthology.

---

# Introduction

*"In the final analysis, it's people—families—who have to make the adjustments. Certainly, the economy of the tobacco-producing states and the large manufacturers will be affected [by the tobacco lawsuits]. But the continuing controversy over tobacco touches the lives of individuals."*

*—Dixie Watts Reaves, associate professor in the College of Agriculture and Life Sciences, and Wayne D. Purcell, professor of agriculture and applied economics and coordinator of the Rural Economic Analysis Program at Virginia Polytechnic Institute and State University in Blacksburg, Virginia*

In August 1995 the *Wall Street Journal* reported: "The Food and Drug Administration—declaring cigarettes a drug—[has just] released research that constitutes one of the most blistering attacks the government has ever made against an industry." That research revealed that tobacco companies had misled the public about the dangerous side effects of smoking. During the next three years, individuals who contracted cancer and other life-threatening diseases linked to cigarettes accused the tobacco industry of lying about the health problems caused by smoking. Those who became ill maintained that tobacco companies had denied that nicotine in tobacco was addictive and that cigarettes were harmful when, in fact, tobacco manufacturers had scientific evidence to the contrary. Few juries actually found the tobacco companies culpable for the smokers' illnesses, however. Nevertheless, tobacco manufacturers soon realized that protracted court fights were expensive and, in an effort to protect themselves from state-level lawsuits, they began negotiations with states. The states wanted enough money to offset their Medicaid costs for smoking-related illnesses, and the tobacco companies wanted assurance that the lawsuits would stop. The resulting agreement was the tobacco Master Settlement Agreement (MSA). According to the terms of the settlement signed in November 1998, the tobacco companies agreed to pay forty-six participating states a total of $206 billion over the following twenty-five years and restrict tobacco advertising directed to youths; the states agreed to prohibit further litigation against tobacco companies. While seemingly a win-win solution, the MSA had some far-reaching and, to some, unthought of adverse consequences. Publicity surrounding the MSA resulted in more public awareness about the dangers associated with smoking and increased societal disapproval of the habit and those involved in the tobacco industry. Tobacco growers as well as manufacturers are now viewed with increasing disdain. This shift in the way tobacco growers are viewed has economic as well as social implications.

The growing evidence of deadly smoking-related health problems that led to strong antitobacco legislation puts economic pressure on tobacco farmers and threatens the existence of many family farms in tobacco-growing states. North Carolina, South Carolina, Kentucky, Tennessee, and Virginia together produce 89 percent of the country's tobacco. The total U.S. tobacco crop—some 1.5 billion pounds in the mid-1990s—generates $2.85 billion in farm revenues for families on 124,000 tobacco farms. A high-value crop, tobacco can bring in gross revenues of over four thousand dollars per acre, allowing farmers to be successful with a small amount of land under cultivation.

The impact of the tobacco settlement on growers has been social as well as economic. Researchers at Wake Forest University Department of Public Health Sciences argue that tobacco is not just a lucrative cash crop; it is part of the cultural heritage of small farmers in the South. Kentucky writer and farmer Wendall Berry insists that when he was a boy, "To be recognized as a tobacco man was to be accorded an honor such as other cultures bestow on the finest hunters or warriors or poets." While tobacco cultivation is economically and culturally important to growers, increasing societal disapproval of smoking has led many farmers to consider other agricultural pursuits.

However, the very profitability of tobacco growing and the fact that it takes proportionately fewer acres to make money growing tobacco than it takes to grow other crops makes it more difficult for farmers to switch. According to North Carolina representative Eva M. Clayton, the average tobacco farm in her state is 172 to 319 acres, compared to 419 acres for the average size farm producing other crops. Clayton maintains that it will take eight acres of cotton, fifteen acres of corn, twenty acres of soybeans, and thirty acres of wheat to equal the income of a single acre of tobacco. Therefore, she contends, even though many farmers would like to grow a crop other than tobacco, the additional land that they need is either unavailable or too expensive to buy. Often, too, land that is suitable for tobacco will not support other crops. Dixie Watts Reaves and Wayne D. Purcell, professors at Virginia Polytechnic Institute and State University, contend, "No crop can be grown on a large scale that comes close to replacing tobacco as a source of family income."

Tobacco growers too discouraged to attempt growing other crops are often forced to get out of farming altogether. However, finding employment in rural areas is often a challenge, and a state-level program of economic development may be required. Reaves and Purcell suggest that state and federal governments increase access to credit for those growers who are transitioning into work other than farming. Moreover, several of the tobacco-producing states are making some of the money from their share of the MSA available to assist growers who are displaced from agricultural employment. For example, North Carolina and Virginia, which received $4.6 billion and $4 billion respectively, have earmarked half of the money they received from the national settlement for communities that are economically dependent on tobacco. Further, as part of the MSA, cigarette companies agreed to pay $5.15 billion over the next twelve years to the National Tobacco Growers' Settlement Trust Fund to compensate tobacco farmers for financial losses resulting from the anticipated decline in cigarette consumption.

Growing tobacco has become an economic and moral problem for farmers in the United States. In the following chapters, authors in *Tobacco and Smoking: Opposing Viewpoints* consider how research on the adverse health effects of smoking has led to many problems and solutions: Is Tobacco Use a Serious Problem? What Factors Contribute to Tobacco Use?

How Can Tobacco Use Be Reduced? Is Tobacco Use a Serious Problem Worldwide? Solutions to tobacco-related problems often have wide-reaching effects as demonstrated by the challenges faced by tobacco growers after the Master Tobacco Settlement of 1998. Indeed, that agreement has forever changed the tenor of debates about tobacco and smoking and greatly impacted businesses and individuals.

# CHAPTER 1

# Is Tobacco Use a Serious Problem?

# Chapter Preface

Since 1964, when Luther L. Terry, then–surgeon general of the United States, issued a report declaring that smoking causes lung cancer and other life-threatening diseases, tobacco use has been recognized in the United States as a serious health risk. In the forty years since the *Surgeon General's Report on Smoking and Health* was released, research has linked smoking to coronary heart disease, serious respiratory problems such as asthma and emphysema, cataracts, and a variety of cancers in addition to lung cancer.

While many men stopped tobacco use as a result of the heightened awareness of tobacco's risks—the percentage of male smokers is almost half of what it was in the 1960s—women have been much slower to respond. Women's smoking has declined by only 35 percent since the 1960s, with lung cancer, once considered exclusively a "man's disease," now the leading cancer killer of women. Further, heart disease kills more women in the United States than any other condition, and research has shown that women who smoke are six times more likely to have a heart attack than those who do not. According to Canadian scientist Pierre Band of Health Canada in Quebec, female smokers—especially those who begin to smoke within five years of puberty, when breasts are developing—also stand an increased risk of breast cancer. The multitude of debilitating and even deadly diseases women can suffer due to smoking make their tobacco use a serious problem.

In addition to the physical harm smoking can do to a woman's body, women who smoke during pregnancy expose their unborn children to the detrimental effects of nicotine as well. According to Duke University pharmacology professor Theodore A. Slotkin, "Nicotine exposure is likely to be the single most widespread prenatal chemical insult in the world, continuing unabated despite decades of educational and medical intervention." Slotkin's research indicates that nicotine acts directly on the fetus's developing brain by interrupting the placental exchange of oxygen, diminishing the nutrient supply to the fetus, and exposing the fetus to carbon monoxide and hydrogen cyanide.

While the effects of tobacco use on women and their unborn children are well known, the reasons why smoking rates for women have not dropped as substantially as have men's rates remain puzzling. Many researchers suggest that aggressive advertising targeted to young girls is responsible. For example, Virginia Slims, the first brand of cigarettes created specifically for young female consumers, was introduced in 1967. By 1973, when smoking initiation for young girls peaked, all the major tobacco companies had at least one brand advertised specifically to women. These ads usually appeared in fashion or teen magazines and linked smoking to sophistication, fashion, and slimness.

While some experts think that cigarette advertising explains women's surprising smoking rates, others believe the reason is related to women's unique physiology. Kenneth Perkins, a researcher at the University of Pittsburgh, suggests that the nicotine in cigarettes affects women differently than it affects men, easing women's stress and anxiety levels more profoundly than it does those of their male counterparts. Moreover, many teen girls and women use smoking as a method of weight control. Michele Bloch, a researcher at the National Institutes of Health, explains: "Cigarettes do depress weight because nicotine increases the metabolism." As Bess H. Marcus, a researcher at Brown University comments, "The three main reasons women smoke are to manage weight, mood, and stress."

The harmful effect of smoking on women's health is just one example of the problems related to tobacco use. Authors in the following chapter debate many others as they explore this important public health issue.

*"Tobacco smoke is even more cancerous than previously thought, for both smokers and nonsmokers who breathe in the fumes, causing cancer in . . . more parts of the body than previously believed."*

# Smoking Is Harmful to Human Health

*Medical Letter on the CDC and FDA*

In the following viewpoint editors from the *Medical Letter on the CDC and FDA* maintain that tobacco smoke is more harmful to human health than previously thought. They argue that it causes cancer in more parts of the body than once believed, and that half of the world's 1.2 billion smokers will die prematurely from cancer, heart disease, emphysema, and other smoking-related diseases. The *Medical Letter on the CDC and FDA* is a newsletter covering the Centers for Disease Control and Prevention's (CDC) involvement with threats to public health and the Federal Drug Administration's (FDA) research on drugs and disease.

As you read, consider the following questions:
1. According to the editors, why do scientists now have a clearer picture of the dangers of tobacco?
2. What do the editors maintain is the best way to prevent deaths from smoking?
3. Exposure to secondhand smoke increases the risk of lung cancer by what percentage, according to the editors?

Medical Letter on the CDC and FDA, "Smoking More Cancerous than Believed, WHO Cancer Experts Say," *Medical Letter on the CDC and FDA*, July 28, 2002.

Tobacco smoke is even more cancerous than previously thought, for both smokers and nonsmokers who breathe in the fumes, causing cancer in many more parts of the body than previously believed, a panel of experts has concluded.

Although smoking has been established as a leading cause of cancer, scientists have only now been able to track more than one generation of smokers to develop a clear picture of the dangers of tobacco.

The scientists, convened by the International Agency for Research on Cancer, a branch of the World Health Organization, said that for types of cancer already known to be caused by smoking, the risk of tumors is even higher than previously noted. The research also definitively proves that secondhand smoke causes cancer.

The analysis is the first major examination of the accumulated research on tobacco smoke and cancer since 1986. A full report of the findings will be published later this year [2002].

The scientists combined the results of more than 3000 studies involving millions of people, which allowed them to draw conclusions not possible in smaller studies.

"We are still learning about just how damaging cigarette smoking is," said the panel's chairman, Dr. Jonathan Samet, head of epidemiology at the Johns Hopkins School of Public Health. "Only now are we beginning to see the full picture of what happens when a generation begins to smoke at an early age, as youth do, and then smoke across their whole lifetime. Before, we only had snapshots."

## Half of All Smokers Die Prematurely

"The full picture is more disturbing than what we saw when we only had the smaller pieces," he said.

There are about 1.2 billion smokers worldwide, half of whom will die prematurely from cancer, heart disease, emphysema or other smoking-related diseases, research has shown.

The best way to prevent those deaths is to get smokers to quit, the scientists said.

"Our group concluded that any possible public health gains from changes in cigarette characteristics or composition would be minimal by comparison. Changes in cigarettes

## Dangers of Smoking

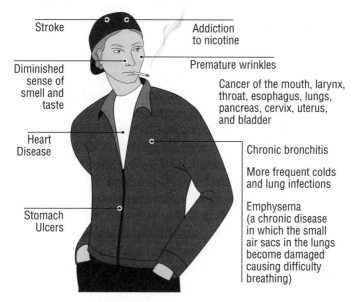

Stroke

Diminished sense of smell and taste

Heart Disease

Stomach Ulcers

Addiction to nicotine

Premature wrinkles

Cancer of the mouth, larynx, throat, esophagus, lungs, pancreas, cervix, uterus, and bladder

Chronic bronchitis

More frequent colds and lung infections

Emphysema (a chronic disease in which the small air sacs in the lungs become damaged causing difficulty breathing)

*Journal of the American Medical Association*, November 3, 1999.

are not the way to prevent cancer," Samet said.

The 29 experts from 12 countries found that in types of cancer already linked to smoking, the risk is even higher than previously believed.

## The Cancer Risk

"For example, for tumors of the bladder and the renal pelvis, previously we thought the elevated risk was maybe three to four times that of a nonsmoker. Today, it looks like the risk is elevated five to six times," said Dr. Paul Kleihues, director of the U.N. cancer research agency.

Two cancer types under suspicion were cleared—those of the breast and endometrium. Prostate cancer has been less studied, but the group did not believe it is caused by smoking.

Types of cancer newly declared to be caused by smoking were cancers of the stomach, liver, cervix, uterus, kidney, nasal sinus and myeloid leukemia.

"It does look as if it's the cancers that are principally caused by hormones that are not affected by smoking. Most of the other cancers throughout the body are induced by exposure to chemicals, often environmental ones," said Sir Richard Doll, an Oxford University professor who was on the panel.

"Practically all the cancers of tissues that are exposed to the environment in one way or another are affected by the chemicals distributed throughout the body when you inhale tobacco smoke," Doll said.

Cancers already identified as being caused by smoking include lung, oral cavity, gullet, larynx, pharynx, pancreas and bladder.

The panel also analyzed 20–30 years of research on cancer and secondhand smoke, and concluded secondhand tobacco smoke increases the risk of lung cancer by 20%.

While some national governments have concluded secondhand smoke causes cancer, this is the first time the U.N. cancer agency—which has strict criteria for evaluating evidence—or any organization with a global sweep has reached this conclusion.

The group found no clear evidence that children exposed to their parents' tobacco smoke in the womb or after birth have an elevated risk of developing childhood cancers. Whether they face an increased risk of lung or other cancer in adulthood remains unclear, the panel said.

*"Damage done from alcohol, damage done
from drugs, from suicide and particularly
from homicide all are vastly more
important than the damage done from
tobacco."*

# The Harmful Effects of
# Smoking Are Exaggerated

Robert A. Levy, interviewed by Stephen Goode

In the following viewpoint, taken from an interview conducted by Stephen Goode, Robert A. Levy maintains that
the federal government has greatly exaggerated the health
risks of smoking. He argues that the government's statistics
are flawed and insists that the damage done by alcohol,
drugs, suicide, and homicide are all more harmful to Americans' health than is the damage done by tobacco. Robert A.
Levy is a fellow at the Cato Institute, a conservative think
tank. Stephen Goode is a writer for *Insight* magazine.

As you read, consider the following questions:
1. According to Robert Levy, which factors, in addition to
   smoking, contribute to smoking-related deaths?
2. In Levy's opinion, why is the corruption of science for
   political ends dangerous?
3. What effect has the exaggeration of smoking risks had
   on public policy, according to Levy?

*Insight: In "Lies, Damned Lies, & 400,000 Smoking-Related Deaths" you concluded that the government's estimate of 400,000 annual deaths due to cigarette smoking is unreliable. What's wrong with that figure?*

Robert A. Levy: According to the Centers for Disease Control and Prevention, tobacco-related diseases are those in which the rate of risk among smokers is higher than among nonsmokers. But epidemiologists will tell you without exception, I think, that "simply higher" is not enough. In most studies, the requirement to show a correlation is that the risk be three or four times as high. The reason for requiring a relative risk rate among smokers of three or four times what it is among nonsmokers before categorizing a disease as smoking-related is that epidemiological studies are subject to all sorts of statistical problems.

There's the problem of sampling error. There is the problem of bias. The third problem is what epidemiologists call "compounding variables": that is the failure to take into account variables that are correlated both with the disease and with smoking. The obvious one in this case is socioeconomic status, as smokers tend to be less affluent than nonsmokers. So because of the problems of sampling, bias and of compounding variables, epidemiologists insist that to categorize a disease as tobacco-related the disease has to have a relative risk among smokers that is three or four times that among nonsmokers.

The relative risk of smoking for many types of heart disease is less than 2-to-1, and if you eliminate even those that are just below 2-to-1 you reduce the estimated number of tobacco-related deaths by about 55 to 60 percent.

We know that smokers are poorer than nonsmokers, have worse nutritional intake, typically have less exercise and less education. Those factors contribute to the contraction of various diseases described as smoking-related. To suggest that the entire incidence among smokers is because these people smoke is to ignore that they share exposure to many other characteristics that also impact health.

## The Risk of Smoking Is Distorted

*What's the reason for the distortion?*

Underlying such manipulation of statistics one often finds

a political agenda, a public-policy agenda, which seeks to convince the public that something is a terrible scourge—and to do so even if the polemic violates the standards and principles of statistics and epidemiology.

This is not to say that tobacco is not a problem. Tobacco is clearly a problem. The evidence is overwhelming that use of tobacco can cause lung cancer, emphysema, bronchitis. But with respect to other diseases its role is less certain. This causes us to ask whether the government is lying to us in presenting these kinds of statistics, because, if it is, that has implications.

*What implications?*

We've seen what happened with antitobacco lawsuits. They've morphed now into antigun litigation. Shortly, it will be the HMOs [health-maintenance organizations] under attack. Who knows what will be next? Fatty foods and alcohol are other obvious candidates for such government-sponsored litigation. The corruption of science for political ends is destructive to a free society and dangerous to citizens who want their government to refrain from activities that intrude upon the rights of people to make their own choices.

Data are being massaged so as to produce outcomes that the litigants find congenial; whether those outcomes are supported by the data is disregarded. I think that's exactly what happened in the tobacco wars.

Tobacco is a problem about which 45 million people decided that it's too dangerous and they quit smoking. For more than 35 years now we've had warnings on every single pack of cigarettes that has been sold legally in the United States. It's a product about which the risks are well-known. Those risks, in fact, have been exaggerated and this has meant that public policy has focused on the unreal, exaggerated risks to the exclusion of some other sources of risk that might better have been targeted.

## Damage from Tobacco Is Not Great

Damage done from alcohol, damage done from drugs, from suicide and particularly from homicide all are vastly more important than the damage done from tobacco, I think. Tobacco is not an intoxicant. It doesn't cause crime except for those people involved in avoiding taxes or regulation of a product whose price has been pushed through the roof by legislation, taxation and regulation. Tobacco doesn't, as do drugs and alcohol, result in spousal abuse and child abuse. It doesn't break up families. It doesn't result in unemployment. Nor does tobacco result in the deaths of young people. Drugs and alcohol, suicide and homicide are killing young people in the prime of life, with decades of life left. The average age of what are called tobacco-related deaths is 72. Those years lost after 72 are important, but they're not so significant, not of the same magnitude, as years lost to the young.

## Most Smokers Do Not Die from Smoking-Related Diseases

The public-health rhetoric often implies that smoking must be daft, because it is deadly. In fact, most smokers (two-thirds or more) do not die of smoking-related disease. They gamble and win. Moreover, the years lost to smoking come from the end of life, when people are most likely to die of something else anyway. [Ex-President] Bill Clinton's mother, who died of cancer at the age of 70 after smoking two packs a day for most of her life, might, as Mr. Clinton notes, have extended her life by not smoking; but she might also have extended it by eating better or exercising more, and in any case she could never have been sure. From a moral point of view smoking is a lot like eating a fatty diet (and note that sticking to a rigorous low-fat diet is at least as hard as quitting nicotine). Smoking may deserve friendly criticism, but it does not warrant moral indignation, any more than skiing does, and no more is it anyone else's affair.

*Economist*, December 20, 1997–January 2, 1998.

*We've had the tobacco wars. What are the gun wars going to be like?*

Well, we're about to find out because there now are about 28 cities that are suing the gun industry. My forecast is that the gun industry will cave. You had the tobacco industry cave and the tobacco industry [is far wealthier] than the gun industry, so the gun folks are likely to come to the negotiating table with the government bearing down very heavily on their necks. Of course, that's the strategy: To coordinate these lawsuits, forget about whether they have any underlying legal merit, and by sheer force and number of the suits coerce a settlement.

*How can the enormous power of government in these cases be brought under control?*

A solution is a "lose-you-pay" system. When the state is a plaintiff in a civil case—and I use the word "state" broadly to encompass government at all levels—we ought to require that it pay if it loses. The government has coercive taxing power behind it [which, for one thing, supplies an almost unlimited supply of funds], so when the government is the plaintiff in a civil case, we need this extra protection against the abuse of the government's power.

*Is there any means to bring under control the huge fees plaintiff lawyers have been getting in these cases?*

Yes. We could prohibit contingency fees for cases when the state is plaintiff. I don't have any objection to contingency fees arranged by private litigants. But when you combine the state as plaintiff and a contingency-fee contract, that is abusive. You can imagine the abuse you would have if you hired an attorney general and paid him for each indictment he got a grand jury to hand down or if you paid state troopers based on how many speeding tickets they handed out. But that's exactly what's happened with private attorneys hired by the state in these civil cases. We've seen legal fees in Texas of $92,000 an hour!

## Lawsuits Eliminate Personal Responsibility

*Meanwhile, we've been eliminating personal responsibility by saying a person's not responsible for his or her own choice to smoke.*

We actually eliminated assumption of risk. In Florida, Maryland and Vermont they did it by statute. They actually said in their statutes that the tobacco industry may not use assumption of risk as a defense. Secondly, they eliminated the rule of causation. The tobacco industry, they said, could not require the states in court to show a link between any smoker's conduct and the disease. The only evidence the states had to produce were these macrostatistics we've talked about showing the higher incidence of various diseases among smokers than nonsmokers. So it was all washed away in one stroke of the pen, all the rules of causation and the assumption of risk.

That is more destructive than the impact of cigarettes themselves! Basically, we're now telling kids two things: First, you can change the rules of the game after the game has begun because all these rules were retroactive. Second, you can go out and engage in risky behavior and if it doesn't turn out like you wanted, you can force the cost onto some third party.

*"Research has linked secondhand smoke to lung cancer, cardiovascular disease, low birth weight, sudden infant death syndrome (SIDS), asthma, bronchitis, pneumonia, middle ear infections, and nasal and eye irritation."*

# Secondhand Smoke Is Harmful to Human Health

Mayo Clinic

Regular exposure to secondhand smoke can threaten the health of nonsmokers, the Mayo Clinic argues in the following viewpoint. It maintains that secondhand smoke irritates the lungs and other tissues and is linked to a variety of diseases including asthma, bronchitis, and lung cancer. Children, the clinic insists, are particularly vulnerable to health threats from secondhand smoke. Low birth weight, sudden infant death syndrome, ear infections, and juvenile asthma are just some of the health problems secondhand smoke causes in children. The Mayo Clinic is a not-for-profit health center based in Rochester, Minnesota.

As you read, consider the following questions:

1. According to the Mayo Clinic, what is sidestream smoke?
2. What is the concentration of cotinine in the blood of twenty-one- to thirty-six-week-old fetuses whose mothers smoke, according to the clinic?
3. How did regular exposure to secondhand smoke affect the health of nurses who took part in a recent study, according to the clinic?

Mayo Clinic, "Secondhand Smoke," www.mayoclinic.com, January 28, 2002. Copyright © 2002 by Mayo Foundation for Medical Education and Research, Rochester, MN 55905. All rights reserved. Reproduced by permission.

A burning cigarette is a health risk to everyone in the same room. The scientific evidence of tobacco hazards is strongest for smokers. However, research reveals that regular exposure to secondhand tobacco smoke also threatens the health of nonsmokers.

Secondhand smoke, also known as environmental tobacco smoke, is a mixture of sidestream smoke from the burning end of a cigarette, pipe or cigar and smoke exhaled from the lungs of smokers. About half the smoke generated from a cigarette is sidestream smoke. Sidestream smoke contains essentially the same compounds as does smoke inhaled by the smoker.

## Secondhand Smoke Is a Health Risk

Secondhand smoke contains substances that irritate the lining of the lung and other tissues. It promotes genetic changes in cells and interferes with cell development, raising the risk of certain cancers.

A 1996 study published in the *Journal of the American Medical Association* found detectable levels of serum cotinine—a breakdown product of nicotine—in nearly 9 of every 10 nonsmokers in a large, nationally representative sample. Researchers also have found that more than 40 percent of children ages 2 months to 11 years lived with at least one smoker.

Research has linked secondhand smoke to lung cancer, cardiovascular disease, low birth weight, sudden infant death syndrome (SIDS), asthma, bronchitis, pneumonia, middle ear infections, and nasal and eye irritation. Children especially are vulnerable.

## Harmful Effects on Children

Children exposed to secondhand smoke have an increased risk of ear infections, wheezing, cough, pneumonia and bronchitis.

Exposure to cigarette smoke begins in the womb. Concentrations of cotinine in the blood of fetuses 21 to 36 weeks old are about 90 percent of levels in the mother's blood. Cotinine is also passed in breast milk. One study found that infants who were exclusively breast-fed by mothers who smoked had urinary cotinine levels in the same range as those of active smokers.

Passive smoke can initiate childhood asthma and has been linked to increased severity of asthma attacks in children. Infants whose mothers smoke during and after pregnancy are three times more likely to die of SIDS than are infants of nonsmoking mothers. One study found that nonsmoking women 30 or older who lived with a smoker had a greater chance of having a premature or underweight baby than those who lived in a smoke-free home.

## Effects of Parental Smoking

A report in the *Archives of Pediatric and Adolescent Medicine* analyzed past studies and estimated that parental smoking accounts for the following in the United States each year:
• Low birth weight—46,000 infants, 2,800 perinatal deaths
• SIDS—2,000 deaths
• Severe lower respiratory infections (bronchiolitis)— 22,000 hospitalizations, 1,100 deaths

| Health Effects Associated with Secondhand Smoke Exposure | |
|---|---|
| Developmental Effects | • Low birth weight or small for gestational age<br>• Sudden Infant Death Syndrome (SIDS) |
| Respiratory Effects | • Acute lower respiratory tract infections in children<br>• Asthma induction and exacerbation in children<br>• Chronic respiratory symptoms in children<br>• Eye and nasal irritation in adults<br>• Middle ear infections in children |
| Carcinogenic Effects | • Lung Cancer<br>• Nasal Sinus Cancer |
| Cardiovascular Effects | • Heart disease mortality<br>• Acute and chronic coronary heart disease morbidity |

National Cancer Institute, *Cancer Facts*, February 14, 2000. www.cis.nci. nih.gov.

31

• Ear infections (otitis media)—3.4 million outpatient visits, 110,000 treatments with insertion of ear tubes (tympanostomy)
  • Asthma—1.8 million outpatient visits, 14 deaths
  • Fire-related injuries—10,000 outpatient visits, 590 hospitalizations, 250 deaths

The respiratory effects of secondhand smoke appear to be more profound for younger children, according to a 2001 report. Among children ages 4 to 6, those with high levels of cotinine were 4.8 times more likely to have had wheezing apart from a cold in the previous year. They were also 5.3 times more likely to have asthma.

The same study found that children with high levels of cotinine had a 1.8 times higher risk of experiencing wheezing apart from a cold and twice the risk of missing 6 or more days of school during the previous year. They also performed worse on lung function tests.

Children whose parents smoked during pregnancy had lower lung function on average. That suggests that exposure to smoke while in the uterus may have long-term effects on lung growth.

## Lung Cancer and Cardiovascular Disorders

The role of secondhand smoke in the development of cancer is controversial. The U.S. Surgeon General, the Environmental Protection Agency (EPA) and the American Lung Association all have concluded that secondhand smoke can cause lung cancer in nonsmokers. However, in 1998 a federal court ruled against an EPA finding that secondhand smoke is a dangerous carcinogen. The EPA has appealed that ruling and awaits a decision.

At least one group of scientists and physicians—the American Council on Science and Health—argues that evidence of a link between secondhand smoke and lung cancer is not as strong as that for a link between secondhand smoke and respiratory disorders.

But, others say, the dispute doesn't mean that people should disregard the warnings.

"The observation that the link between secondhand smoke and lung cancer may be less firm than for respiratory disorders does not diminish the gravity of the issue or alter the basic public health approaches which are needed," says J. Richard Hickman, M.D., a specialist in preventive medicine at Mayo Clinic, Rochester, Minn.

Researchers are gathering evidence of the effect of secondhand smoke on the heart and blood vessels. A small Japanese study looked at the effects of secondhand smoke on circulation in young men. Exposure to secondhand smoke was associated with reduced blood flow through the arteries feeding the heart. One theory behind the finding is that secondhand smoke affects the function of the cells that line the heart and blood vessels. A study of Swedish women and men ages 45 to 70 found a higher risk of nonfatal heart attack among those whose spouses smoked 20 or more cigarettes a day than among people who were not exposed to secondhand smoke from their spouses. The risk was higher for women.

A study of 32,000 women who were nurses found that regular exposure to secondhand smoke doubled their risk of a heart attack. The study compared outcomes among nurses who reported regular exposure to secondhand smoke at work and home with those who reported no exposure. The study found the association between heart attacks and secondhand smoke after accounting for many other cardiovascular risk factors such as high blood pressure or high cholesterol.

*"There is no evidence at all that breathing so-called secondhand smoke is injurious. . . . This whole business is some sort of superstition."*

# The Harmful Effects of Secondhand Smoke Are Exaggerated

Jeffrey Hart

Secondhand smoke is not harmful to human health, Jeffrey Hart claims in the following viewpoint. He argues that a 1993 Environmental Protection Agency (EPA) report claiming that inhalation of secondhand smoke causes three thousand deaths per year was based on corrupt science. Further, tests on 173 bartenders and waiters failed to show any ill effects from secondhand smoke, he claims. Hart also contends that a ten-year World Health Organization (WHO) study of twenty-one countries found no connection between secondhand smoke and cancer. Jeffrey Hart is a senior editor for the *National Review* and a syndicated columnist.

As you read, consider the following questions:

1. According to Jeffrey Hart, what did the EPA do when it did not get the expected results from secondhand smoke studies?
2. What harm is antismoking zealotry doing, in Hart's opinion?
3. Upon what is the fear of secondhand smoke based, according to the author?

S omething is way out of control on tobacco.
A town named Norwich in Vermont . . . is an upscale town full of Dartmouth professors, physicians, lawyers and so on. Needless to say, Norwich is very liberal. Behind the post office there's a parking lot. And in the parking lot there's one of those NO SMOKING signs, a red circle around a picture of a cigarette with a red bar across the cigarette. This is outdoors! In the parking lot!

In New York City [in 2001], a politician named Peter Vallone is running for mayor. He has proposed measures that, if adopted, will ban smoking in all restaurants and saloons. Period.

Yet there is no evidence at all that breathing so-called secondhand smoke is injurious. No evidence. None. This whole business is some sort of superstition. The City Council, which is on the edge of passing the draconian measures, has not bothered to study the evidence concerning secondhand smoke.

## The 1993 EPA Report

The belief that secondhand smoke is a killer derives from a 1993 statement by the Environmental Protection Agency [EPA] that passive inhaling of smoke causes 3,000 deaths per year in America. This statement was seized upon to justify an anti-smoking rampage. My good friend and columnist Sidney Zion has pointed out that no one bothered to notice that the EPA did not conduct its own study, but rather depended on 11 studies conducted by various groups around the country. When 10 of the 11 failed to deliver the results the EPA wanted, the EPA simply changed the statistical requirements and came up with one out of the 11 that seemed to indicate negative results from secondhand smoke.

Two years later, according to Zion, the Congressional Research Service, an independent agency of Congress, found that there is no scientific evidence that passive smoke is injurious to health.

"In 1998, the World Health Organization," writes Zion, "after a study that covered 21 countries over 10 years at a cost of millions, found no connection between passive smoke and cancer. The WHO . . . buried this report, but it came out in London.

"Shortly after the WHO study, federal judge William Osteen of North Carolina completely destroyed the EPA findings as 'corrupt science.' Don't let his state bother you—Osteen happens to be an anti-tobacco jurist."

## "No Harm at All"

Zion also cites Knoxville, Tenn., where in the summer of 1996–1997 "173 bartenders and waiters were wired to discover the effects on them of secondhand smoke. The results: nothing, no harm at all. Yeah. You could look it up."

If the Vallone anti-smoking measures pass, Mayor Rudolph Giuliani threatens to veto them. There is also talk that he might set up a commission to investigate the scientific evidence regarding secondhand smoke. Vallone never thought of doing that.

I was told a good story by Zion recently. He was standing at the tiny bar on the second floor of Sardi's famous restaurant in the theater district. The bar is so small that only about 10 people can stand at it, and it's always crowded. Next to him stood a woman soaked in the most abominable perfume. Sidney, as is his custom, lit a large cigar. The man with the woman tapped him on the shoulder: "Would you please put out that cigar?" Sidney: "She takes a shower, I put out the cigar."

---

### Secondhand Smoke Is Not a Killer

The role of ETS [Environmental Tobacco Smoke] in the development of chronic diseases like cancer and heart disease is uncertain and controversial. To state that occupational exposure of bartenders is the "#1 killer in the American workplace" is without scientific basis.

Elizabeth M Whelan, American Council on Science and Health, August 1, 2000. www.acsh.org.

---

Of course I'm not saying that smoking is harmless. King James I of England wrote a pamphlet against smoking early in the 17th century. When I was a child, cigarettes were referred to as coffin nails. When I was a junior tennis player, Richard "Pancho" Gonzales told me that he had quit smoking—because cigarette smoke impaired his vision, and at that level of tennis, perfect vision is a necessity. And science since has shown that smoking correlates with lung cancer, not to mention emphysema and other ailments.

But the state of the evidence at the present time indicates that secondhand smoke is harmless. I notice that in its 1993 pronouncement, the EPA claimed 3,000 deaths annually as due to secondhand smoke. Even if that were on the level, it would be fewer than die in bicycle accidents. To be consistent, the abolitionists ought to ban bicycles.

And the anti-smoking zealotry is doing some damage. Even with the regulations as they are now in New York City, some restaurants are going out of business because their floor plan does not permit the isolation of smokers. The famous P.J. Clarke's in midtown Manhattan is on the edge of bankruptcy for that reason. Smoking is allowed at Yankee Stadium only in the private luxury boxes. Impressionistic evidence indicates that the tourist industry is being hurt. Can you tell a Frenchman or a Japanese not to smoke?

## Political Correctness Is to Blame

Now, since the fear of secondhand smoke is based on nothing, where is the frenzy coming from?

I began with that outdoor anti-smoking sign in the parking lot over in Norwich. The citizens there are wealthy, liberal, educated and certainly not stupid.

The problem is, they particularly enjoy looking upon themselves as virtuous. Political correctness, for example, makes them feel virtuous. Sniffing out "racism" somewhere makes them feel virtuous. If they can pin someone as "homophobic," that makes them feel virtuous. Virtue, to be really enjoyable, requires sinners. So the secondhand-smoke scare came as a bonanza. There were scaly, fork-tailed sinners everywhere. And by passing enough tough laws, you could make them virtuous, too.

Of course, they don't want to hear about science, about evidence. You would be attacking a grand opportunity for cheap, and deeply satisfying, virtue.

*"Smoking is one of the riskiest behaviors a kid can indulge in—it's just that the life-threatening dangers don't stare a parent in the face right away."*

# Tobacco Use Among Teens Is a Serious Problem

Susan Dominus

In the following viewpoint Susan Dominus argues that smoking is one of the riskiest behaviors a teenager can indulge in, although the life-threatening dangers might not be immediately obvious to the teens or their parents. She claims that over two thousand young people start smoking each day and a large number of them will die prematurely from smoking-related diseases. Dominus contends that the younger children are when they start smoking, the more likely they are to develop lung cancer later in life. Susan Dominus is a freelance writer, contributing editor for *Glamour* magazine, and a contributing writer for the *New York Times Sunday Magazine*.

As you read, consider the following questions:
1. According to Dominus, what percentage of teens say they smoke?
2. What are two reasons teens often give for starting to smoke, in the author's opinion?
3. What reason does Dominus give to explain the rise in convenience store promotions of tobacco?

Susan Dominus, "Teens and Tobacco: A Love Story," *Good Housekeeping*, vol. 235, November 2002, pp. 118–26. Copyright © 2002 by Good Housekeeping. Reproduced by permission of the author.

The town of Rye, in New York's Westchester County, has a small-town sweetness to it, with an old-fashioned amusement park and a pretty, tree-lined main street. TD's Rye Smoke Shop, located on a central corner, is one of the best-preserved throwbacks to past times, a dimly lit but homey place where kids clamor for dime candy, licorice, and dipsticks.

TD's also sells cigarettes and cigars, though not to kids under 18, in accordance with New York State law. But that doesn't stop them from finding cigarettes elsewhere. Across the street at Starbucks, almost every afternoon, you see 14-, 15-, and 16-year-olds approach one another, asking for a smoke, for a lighter, for another cigarette. It's their way of saying hello, of gaining entree. "Everyone smokes," says Candace, an open-faced 17-year-old enjoying a sunny Friday afternoon on a shop stoop. "Kids in every clique—jocks, preps, goths. . . ."

Compared with drug or alcohol abuse, smoking may seem like the least of a parent's worries, a relatively controlled way for a child to let off some steam or exert her independence. And yet, smoking is one of the riskiest behaviors a kid can indulge in—it's just that the life-threatening dangers don't stare a parent in the face right away. With every study, the news gets more grim. The younger a child starts smoking, for example, the more likely she is to end up with lung cancer, according to recent research from the Harvard School of Public Health—and not just because of the cumulative impact. The younger the smoker, says the study, the more stubborn the carcinogenic buildup that damages DNA and is a precursor to tumor growth; the change starts early and is irreversible.

## The Fastest-Growing Group of Smokers

More than one quarter of all teens say they smoke today. That number is slightly lower than it was five years ago. Yet each day, over 2,000 young people still dabble with smoking for the first time, and a substantial number of them will eventually die of a smoking-related disease. Young adults ages 18 to 24 are also the fastest-growing group of smokers.

So why do kids light up in the first place?

"Some friends of mine in seventh grade just said, 'Why don't we try it?'" says Paul, now a sophomore. His arm draped around Candace, he's wearing cargo pants and is halfway through a cigarette. He's going to be handsome one day, but right now he's skinny, with a rash of acne across his chin only partly disguised by some sparse stubble. He holds a pack of Camels prominently in his hand, like a talisman, turning it upside down, tapping it on the sidewalk like a toy. "I thought, Well, if it's so bad for you, and people do it anyway, there must be something really great about it, right?"

Paul is in a band that's playing later at the town rec hall, and whenever a friend walks by, he calls after him, "See you tonight, right?" Every so often he coughs, making a harsh hacking sound. "I'm the sickliest kid," he admits. But he shrugs when asked if he's worried about getting seriously sick in the future, possibly as a result of smoking. "I'm not afraid of cancer," he says. "I believe in living fast and dying young."

"It's horrible," says Candace. "But there's something so sexy about cigarettes." Her face gets dreamy. "I like it when guys light a cigarette with a match and then flick it away. It's so destructive—so bad boy."

## Weight Control and Smoking

A familiar association. In fact, teenagers smoke for some of the same reasons they always have: It looks cool and they identify it with rebellion. And knowing the risks, as kids now do, may only enhance the appeal. But there's more to it than that. In addition to the old temptations to smoke, kids today have a constellation of reasons that are unique to their generation.

Ever since the introduction of Virginia Slims in 1968, the tobacco industry has lured women with the promise that they could smoke their way to a thinner body. Young women worrying about their weight is nothing new, but the worrying begins earlier these days, fed by a barrage of media images. "I see kids experiencing this pressure to look like the successful people they see on TV, which for teenage girls, means the actresses on *Friends* [a popular TV sitcom], for example," says Michael Levine, a professor of psychology at Ohio's Kenyon College, who specializes in body image and eating disorders. The current fashions for young girls—baby tees, belly-baring halter tops, spaghetti-strap tanks—flaunt more of their bodies, which means more self-scrutiny and, inevitably, self-criticism sooner. Given these pressures, smoking may seem like a quick fix, a diet trick that girls are afraid to go without.

Lisa, a blue-eyed, honey-haired girl with someone's phone number scrawled in pink on her arm, swings by the stoop, Gap bag in hand, to say hi to Candace. "She smokes, and she's an athlete," says Candace, pointing at Lisa. In fact, Lisa explains, she just stopped playing basketball this year and found herself adrift. For comfort, "it was either food or cigarettes, and I chose cigarettes because I didn't want to get gigantic."

Her parents, both overweight and longtime smokers, recently lost more than 20 pounds each. They dieted, "but the smoking helped," according to their daughter. "They're afraid to quit, because they're afraid they'll gain the weight back." Given that the children of smokers are more likely to smoke themselves, Lisa's habit—by now, an addiction, she says with resignation—almost seems inevitable.

Rather than trying to free girls from concerns about their looks, a number of state-supported antismoking campaigns advise parents to work that angle—and point out that smoking, while it may depress weight, also leads to more wrinkles and sallow skin. "I try to appeal to my daughter's vanity," says Megan Powers, a mother of four from Westchester County, referring to her oldest daughter, Colette. "I tell her, 'It makes your teeth yellow, it makes your fingers yellow.'"

## Teens' Parents Are Often Smokers

The family's relationship to cigarettes is a complicated one. Colette, now 20, started smoking with friends about four years ago, but as she puts it, "My dad always smoked, so my parents couldn't get too mad." Ironically, Colette says that smoking actually helped her to create a bond with her father. During a difficult time for the family—she and her parents were arguing constantly over her failure to call when she stayed out late—Colette says there was only one time when she could open up to her father: when the two lit up together on the porch. Though both parents disapproved of her smoking, her mother sensed that it wouldn't help to force the issue. "Was I going to ground her for smoking?" Megan Powers asks rhetorically. "No."

In the past six months or so, Colette has been getting along better with her parents and is happier overall; though still living at home, she's attending college nearby. She hasn't given up smoking yet, but she's smoking less, she says, and she intends to quit soon—partly because she's noticed she has less energy, but also because she's seen through her father how hard it can be to shake the habit once you get older.

---

## The Teen Hooked on Nicotine Checklist (HONC)

1) Have you ever tried to quit, but couldn't?

2) Do you smoke now because it is really hard to quit?

3) Have you ever felt like you were addicted to tobacco?

4) Do you ever have strong cravings to smoke?

5) Have you ever felt like you really needed a cigarette?

6) Is it hard to keep from smoking in places where you are not supposed to, like school?

When you tried to stop smoking . . . (or, when you haven't used tobacco for a while . . . )

7) Did you find it hard to concentrate because you couldn't smoke?

8) Did you feel more irritable because you couldn't smoke?

9) Did you feel a strong need or urge to smoke?

10) Did you feel nervous, restless or anxious because you couldn't smoke?

Elpidoforos S. Soterides et al., *Journal of School Health*, April 2003.

---

Megan Powers's decision to tread lightly with Colette may have been the best tactic under the circumstances. Taking harsh measures with teens can easily backfire, according to Cheryl Healton, president of the American Legacy Foundation, a nonprofit public health organization. Healton suggests playing on a teenager's natural altruism instead. "Point out that even though they may not care about themselves, they're also hurting their friends, even their pets," she says, citing a study that found that cats in smokers' homes were far more likely to develop cancer than cats in tobacco-free homes. "And teenagers also like to get mad, so give them something to get mad about—those tobacco executives whose interest is not your kids' health but their own wealth."

A parent has to be creative, she adds, and tailor an approach for her own kid. Ruth Wooden's son, John, now 18, started to smoke when he was 14, stopped when he was 15, then picked up the habit again at 16. A former smoker herself, Wooden told John how incredibly hard it had been for her to quit, "and the amazing feeling of power I got when I finally did." Her son, she says, "responded to the challenge." When he was 17, around the same time he started taking fitness seriously, John quit again. "He says he can't imagine ever smoking again," his mother maintains.

## Teens Smoke to Be Cool

At 2:20 on an uncharacteristically warm Thursday afternoon in Seattle, the crowd lining the driveway of a sprawling high school is thinning out, leaving behind a core group of 20 or so kids. There's something clannish-looking about them as they bow toward each other almost ritualistically, lighting one another's cigarettes, then stand up and blow smoke off to the side. "Yeah, we're the popular clique," says Kristin, a freckled girl in a striped halter top, her strawberry-blond hair pulled back in a ponytail. "You start smoking to be cool, and then you get addicted," she says matter-of-factly. Her ex-boyfriend, now close buddy Rob, a tall varsity football and basketball player who also smokes, nods in agreement.

There are thousands of miles between home-of-grunge Seattle and New York's Rye, and Kristin's view of cigarettes seems to reflect that distance. Asked if weight control has anything to do with why she smokes, she looks like she's been asked whether she thinks smoking might make her turn purple. "No," she says, "that's not really our thing here."

Kristin argues that kids smoke because they're so independent—which means more responsibility and stress, less parental control. "I tell my parents what I'm doing, not the other way around," she says. "I go to high school, I'm going to night school for college credit, and I have a waitressing job; I earn my own spending money. Sometimes you just need a cigarette." Kristin is not unusual: 55 percent of 12th graders now work three hours or more on a typical school day, according to one survey. Combining a job with the typical pressures of school and adolescence boosts a student's stress level; the extra income gives them the cash they need to buy the cigarettes that seem to calm them down. Nicotine relieves anxiety in adults and has the same calming effect on kids. "Twenty-five years ago, we thought the main reason kids smoked was because of peer pressure," says Edwin Fisher, Ph.D., a professor of psychology, medicine, and pediatrics at Washington University, in St. Louis. "We now understand that the effects of nicotine in raising mood and lowering anxiety are important for teens as well as for adults."

## Teens Smoke to Relieve Stress

Although every era has its anxieties, the stresses on the average teenager today seem more numerous—and possibly more disturbing. "I think there's a sense of our world feeling less safe for everyone, but teens feel those shifts more acutely," says Nadine Kaslow, a professor and chief psychologist at Emory University, in Atlanta, who specializes in adolescence and families. "Yes, there are more teens working, but there's also a higher divorce rate, more violence that they see on television and in movies, and absolutely more violence in everyday life. And kids don't have good ways to regulate their feelings. So they turn to cigarettes for that."

Some antitobacco activists pay close attention to studies that identify kids who are at high risk for smoking, so they can throw them off course. Kids suffering from depression, for example, are more receptive to tobacco advertising and more likely to experiment, according to researchers at the University of Pennsylvania/Georgetown University Transdisciplinary Tobacco Use Research Center. And several studies have established that kids who have attention deficit disorder are twice as likely to start smoking as those who don't. In one of the more aggressive measures under way, Timothy Wilens, M.D., director of substance-abuse services in the pediatric psychopharmacology unit at Massachusetts General Hospital, in Boston, has started a trial in which kids with attention deficit disorder who don't already smoke are prescribed Zyban—which can function as either an antidepressant or a smoking-cessation medication—to stop them from ever starting. "It could have a great combination effect," Dr. Wilens says.

In 1998, the major tobacco companies reached a settlement with the attorneys general of 46 states; among the provisions was a ban on cigarette advertising on billboards and on marketing directly to kids—including in magazines read primarily by young people. But despite the restrictions, tobacco marketing inexorably marches on, with manufacturers ingeniously slipping ads into new places sure to target brand-conscious kids. "When the billboards came down, you saw increases in promotions at places like convenience stores," says Danny McGoldrick, director of research at the Washington, D.C.-based Campaign for Tobacco-Free Kids. "We know that 75 percent of kids visit convenience stores at least once a week, so they're still getting bombarded." According to the Centers for Disease Control and Prevention, cigarette displays appear in 92 percent of the stores located in communities around public schools; other recent polls have found kids more likely than adults to be exposed to cigarette advertising.

## Strong Anti-Smoking Message

But the anti-smoking lobby has grown more sophisticated about its own marketing techniques, creating television ads using kids to show kids that smoking isn't cool—rather than adults lecturing them about the dangers. The American Legacy Foundation's Truth Campaign, for example, created a series of television ads that appeal to kids' sense of the subversive, pitting them against the industry suits trying to make a buck at their expense. The foundation placed the commercials nationally, choosing edgy programming— "*MTV* or wrestling, not *Seventh Heaven*," says American Legacy's Healton. The Truth Campaign spots have started to make an impression, according to the Research Triangle Institute, which conducted a phone survey of 15,000 randomly selected teens and queried them about which commercials they'd seen, as well as about their smoking habits.

(The findings were published in the *American Journal of Public Health*.)

Along with savvy advertising, hard-hitting legislative policies are chipping away at kids' inclination to smoke: In Florida, teens under 18 caught with cigarettes may find themselves losing their driver's license or facing steep fines, rather than just getting a warning from Mom. And in states like New York and California, legislators have recently imposed steep taxes on cigarettes—New York now charges $7 a pack, the highest price in the nation—which is expected to inhibit some teens from taking up the habit.

## Teens Plan to Quit Smoking

But it's those already addicted who are hardest to reach. It is evening now in Rye, New York, and Paul is standing on the lawn outside the rec hall, where he has just played acoustic guitar with his band. "Yeah, I sucked tonight," he says, smoking a cigarette with two friends. The group is asked if higher cigarette prices make a difference to them. "Not really," says Emily, a pack-a-day 17-year-old who lost her grandfather to lung cancer. "It just means that if I have to make a choice between spending my money on cigarettes or food, I'll skip the food." Paul confessed he'd take the cash from his parents' wallets for cigarettes, sticking to singles so they wouldn't notice.

The good news is that to some extent, almost every kid I spoke to is already halfway there: They all say they plan on quitting eventually.

"I definitely don't plan on being one of those yucky mommies you see rolling their kid in a stroller while they're sucking on some nasty cigarette," says Kristin, the Seattle high school student. "I mean, I know I'm going to stop."

Has she ever tried seriously to quit? "Oh, yeah," she says. And was she successful? She rolls her eyes as only a teenager can, though it's unclear who, or what, is annoying her. "No," she says finally. "I guess I wasn't."

*"Between 2001 and 2002, the proportion of teens saying that they had ever smoked cigarettes fell by 4 or 5 percentage points in each grade surveyed."*

# Tobacco Use Among Teens Is Declining

*Cancer Weekly*

Teen smoking has been dropping steadily since it reached peak rates in 1996 and 1997, the editors of *Cancer Weekly* contend in the following viewpoint. According to the editors, between 2001 and 2002, the proportion of teens who said they had ever smoked declined by four or five percentage points in grades eight, ten, and twelve. The editors contend that several factors—including increasing cigarette prices, less advertising that reaches young people, more antismoking ads, and a great deal of negative publicity about smoking—could be responsible for the decrease. *Cancer Weekly* is a newsletter that reports on the latest oncology developments.

As you read, consider the following questions:

1. According to the editors, why do researchers expect fewer smokers in the upper grades over the next few years?
2. Why have cigarette prices increased since 1998, in the editors' opinion?
3. In what ways have teens' opinions of smoking become more negative, according to the editors?

American young people are turning away from cigarette smoking at a pace that should bring cheer to parents, educators, and health professionals alike. Teen use of cigarettes has been dropping steadily and substantially since the peak rates in 1996 and 1997.

Between 2001 and 2002, the proportion of teens saying that they had ever smoked cigarettes fell by 4 or 5 percentage points in each grade surveyed (8, 10, and 12)—more than in any recent year.

"I cannot overemphasize how important these developments are to the health and longevity of this generation of young people," said Lloyd Johnston, principal investigator of the study and lead author of the forthcoming report with fellow social psychologists Patrick O'Malley and Jerald Bachman. "Smoking remains the leading preventable cause of premature death and disease in this country. Therefore, significant reductions in smoking translate into a great many lives lengthened and an even larger number of serious illnesses prevented—including heart disease, stroke, cancer and emphysema."

The Monitoring the Future study is funded by the U.S. National Institute on Drug Abuse under research grants made to the University of Michigan Institute for Social Research. It began in 1975 and has tracked the smoking habits of high school seniors in the country each year since then. Grades 8 and 10 were added in 1991 and have been surveyed annually along with the 12th graders for the past 12 years. The 2002 survey results are based on about 44,000 students in nearly 400 randomly selected public and private secondary schools from across the continental United States.

## Smoking Rates Are Down by Half

Following the recent peak in 1996, smoking rates for 8th graders have dropped by half. Current smoking (any use in the past 30 days) fell from 21% to 10.7%; current daily smoking fell from 10.4% to 5.1%; and current half-pack-a-day smoking fell from 4.3% to 2.1%. Among 10th graders, rates have dropped by nearly half, and among 12th graders by about a quarter to a third. Although proportional declines have been smaller in the upper grades, the investigators expect that picture to improve during the next few years, simply as a result of the current 8th graders becoming older. "There are a number of potential explanations for these important declines in teen smoking," Johnston said. "These include increasing prices, less tobacco advertising that reaches young people, more antismoking ads, and a lot more negative publicity about the tobacco industry." Some of these changes originated with the tobacco settlement between the state attorneys general and the industry. Certain forms of advertising, such as billboard advertising and the Joe Camel ads, were withdrawn as one of the conditions of the settlement.

The American Legacy Foundation was created with funds from the settlement, and one of its activities was to launch a major antismoking campaign aimed at youth. Tobacco companies have raised their cigarette prices to help pay for the settlement; moreover, a number of states have raised cigarette taxes, which also translates into higher prices.

"There is good evidence from a number of studies, including this one, that higher prices help to deter youth smoking, so we think that price has been one important factor," Johnston said. (One such study of price effects, funded by the Robert Wood Johnson Foundation, used data from the Monitoring the Future study.) "But in addition, there have been some important changes in how young people view smoking."

One important change has been a substantial increase, beginning in 1996, in the proportion of young people who perceive regular smoking as dangerous. That upturn in perceived risk was followed a year later (beginning in 1997) by an upturn in disapproval of smoking as well as by the beginning of the downturn in actual teen smoking.

## Teens Recognize the Risks

The proportion of 8th graders saying that a person runs a "great risk" of harming himself physically or in other ways by being a pack-a-day smoker increased steadily from 50% in 1995 to 59% in 2000, before stabilizing. The proportion of them disapproving pack-a-day smoking rose from 77% to 85% between 1996 and 2002, while over the same interval the proportion saying that they smoked at least once in the prior 30 days (current smoking) fell from 21% to 11%. In 2000 there was a particularly large increase at all three grade levels in the perceived risk of smoking. "That corresponds to when the American Legacy Foundation's 'truth' campaign against smoking was launched," Johnston said, "so we think it quite possible that this campaign played a role in changing that belief among teens. We also saw a sharp increase in youth exposure to antismoking ads that year, which helps to confirm that hypothesis. But clearly things were headed in the right direction even before that campaign got started, so it can account for only part of the downturn."

## Teenage Smoking Continues to Decline

Use of cigarettes by American teenagers decreased from 2000 to 2001 according to the annual Monitoring the Future Survey released today by the Department of Health and Human Services [HHS]. This decline, observed for 8th and 10th graders, continues a decreasing trend begun around 1996. Decreases have also been found for seniors in recent years. These reductions in teenage smoking come on the heels of increases from the early to mid-1990s and are excellent news in the nation's battle to reduce the toll exacted by this leading cause of preventable death and disease. . . .

"The finding that fewer teenagers are smoking is very encouraging as more teens are making smart choices that will help them avoid tobacco-related health threats," said HHS Secretary Tommy G. Thompson. "Overall, drug use among America's teenagers has remained level or declined for the fifth year in a row, and that's good news."

U.S. Department of Health and Human Services, December 19, 2001.

Young people in middle and high school have clearly become less accepting of cigarette smoking, and that trend continued in 2002. The younger students are the least accepting of smoking, with 85% of the 8th graders in 2002 saying they disapprove of someone smoking at a pack-a-day level, compared with 81% of the 10th graders and 74% of the 12th graders. But the 8th graders are the least aware of the dangers of cigarette use. Only 58% of them, even in 2002, think there is great risk associated with pack-a-day smoking, compared with 74% of the 12th graders, for example.

## Negative Attitudes

The Monitoring the Future study tracks a number of other specific attitudes about smoking and smokers, and the investigators report that a number of these attitudes have become more negative in recent years. For example, students in all three grade levels are becoming less accepting of being around smokers. Currently about half of them express that view. The proportion of 8th graders who agree with the statement "I strongly dislike being near people who are smoking" increased from 46% in 1996 to 54% in 2002. (Among 10th graders the increase was from 42% in 1997 to 49% in 2002; and among 12th graders from 38% to 47% over the same interval.) These changes all are statistically significant.

An increasing proportion of young people are also coming to see smoking as reflecting poor judgment on the part of their peers who smoke. Some 64% of the 8th graders now agree with the statement "I think that becoming a smoker reflects poor judgment," as do about 60% of the 10th- and 12th graders.

But perhaps of most importance to teens is how their peers feel about dating someone who smokes. The proportions saying that they prefer to date non-smokers rose to 81% of 8th graders by 2002 (up from 71% in 1996), 76% of 10th graders (up from 68% in 1997), and 72% of 12th graders (up from 64% in 1997). This aversion to dating smokers is about equally strong among males and females.

"It now appears that taking up smoking makes a youngster less attractive to the great majority of the opposite sex," Johnston concluded, "just the opposite of what cigarette advertising has been promising all these years. I think this is something that teens need to know, because it may be the most compelling argument for why they should abstain from smoking or, for that matter, quit if they have already started."

## Cigarettes Are Easily Available

Efforts to reduce youth access to cigarettes, begun by the FDA some years ago and continued by a number of states and localities, appear to have had some success. The proportion of 8th graders saying it would be "fairly easy" or "very easy" to get cigarettes if they wanted them has fallen from 77% in 1996 to 64% in 2002, while the comparable proportion for 10th graders fell from 91% to 83% over the same interval. Both grades showed a significant decline in perceived availability in 2002, specifically.

"It is worth noting that the great majority of youngsters this age still think they can get cigarettes, if they want them," Johnston said. "Despite the progress, we still have a fair way to go."

Monitoring the Future has been funded under a series of competing, investigator-initiated research grants from the National Institute on Drug Abuse. Surveys of nationally representative samples of American high school seniors were begun in 1975, making the class of 2002 the 28th such class surveyed. Surveys of 8th- and 10th graders were added to the design in 1991, making the 2002 nationally representative samples the 12th such classes surveyed. The sample sizes in 2002 are 15,500 8th graders, 14,700 10th graders, and 13,500 12th graders, for a total of 43,700 students. They are located in 394 private and public secondary schools across the coterminous United States, selected with probability proportionate to size, to yield nationally representative samples of students in each of the three grade levels.

*"A single dip of spit tobacco has as much as four times the amount of nicotine as a single cigarette."*

# Smokeless Tobacco Use Is Harmful to Human Health

Robert Preidt

In the following viewpoint Robert Preidt maintains that people who consider smokeless (spit) tobacco less harmful than cigarettes are dangerously misinformed. He argues that spit tobacco causes cavities, gum disease, and cancer. Further, spit tobacco users get four times as much nicotine in one dip of tobacco as smokers get in one cigarette. Thus, spit tobacco users become addicted much faster. Preidt argues that young people are attracted to the habit because sports figures often use spit tobacco. Experts estimate that as many as 20 percent of high school boys are regular users. Robert Preidt is a reporter for HealthScout.com, a consumer health Web site.

As you read, consider the following questions:
1. According to the author, how many Americans use spit tobacco?
2. Why does spit tobacco contain silica, in Preidt's opinion?
3. What percentage of major league ballplayers does the author report use spit tobacco?

Robert Preidt, "Chew on This: Experts Say Spit Tobacco Causes Gum Disease, Oral Cancer," *University of Maryland National Health News*, March 11, 2001. Copyright © 2001 by University of Maryland Medical System. Reproduced by permission.

You can call it dip, chew, smokeless or snuff. Just make sure you dub spit tobacco dangerous.

Too many people believe spit or chewing tobacco is a safer alternative to cigarettes, experts say.

But that's a potentially deadly misconception, says Joan McGowan, an associate professor of dental hygiene at the University of Michigan.

"You're getting many of the same poisons and cancer-causing agents in the spit tobacco products as you do with the smoking. It's true that you don't inhale with the spit tobacco, but your chances for oral cancer are greatly increased, plus it really does a number on your teeth, your gums and the bone that holds your teeth in your mouth," McGowan says. "It's still the same tobacco that is used [in cigarettes], with all the curatives put in it and all the things to process it, and so it's really very dangerous."

It's estimated that 10 million to 16 million Americans use spit tobacco.

If the threat of cancer isn't enough to stop you from using spit tobacco, here's something else to chew on. It contains silica, a finely ground sand that abrades the soft tissue in your mouth.

"The rationale is to rough up the gum tissues so that your tissues bleed, which allows the nicotine from the tobacco quicker entry into your bloodstream," McGowan says.

That silica also grinds or flattens the enamel of your teeth.

## Smokeless Tobacco Causes Cavities, Gum Disease, and Cancer

McGowan is coordinator for the Michigan coalition of Oral Health America's National Spit Tobacco Education Program (NSTEP), a campaign to reduce spit tobacco use, especially among children.

The U.S. Department of Health and Human Services (HHS) says as many as 20 percent of high school boys use spit tobacco.

NSTEP wants to convince young people not to pick up the spit tobacco habit. McGowan says a single dip of spit tobacco has as much as four times the amount of nicotine as a single cigarette.

"So you're getting a lot more [nicotine] faster and you become addicted quicker," she says.

One of the main targets of NSTEP is the baseball industry, long associated with spit tobacco. Children see their heroes chewing a wad of tobacco on the field and want to emulate them.

---

## Spit Tobacco Widely Used by Male Athletes

Although spit tobacco is often marketed as "smokeless tobacco," implying that it poses fewer health risks than cigarettes, chewing tobacco and snuff are highly addictive and can lead to oral cancer, mouth lesions, and gum disease. Male athletes are particularly at risk, chiefly because of intensive marketing targeted to adolescent boys, distribution of free spit tobacco to college players, promotions by professional athletes, and the convenience of using spit tobacco during games.

A national study found spit tobacco to be widely used among male college athletes, especially baseball players. Fully 41 percent of baseball players and 29 percent of football players had used spit tobacco in the previous 12 months. These figures are a drop from nearly 60 percent of baseball players and 40 percent of football players in the early 1990s, yet they still dwarf the national use rate of 17 percent for college men.

In most women's sports, spit tobacco use is rare, but in the same national study, nearly 18 percent of women skiers reported using.

A survey of varsity baseball and football players at 16 California colleges found clear racial and ethnic differences in spit tobacco use: 48 percent of Native American athletes, 44 percent of whites, 33 percent of both Hispanics and Asians, and 11 percent of African Americans use spit tobacco. Almost 98 percent of the athletes who use spit tobacco started by the age of 20.

Higher Education Center for Alcohol and Other Drug Prevention, March 21, 2002. www.edc.org.

---

NSTEP has a representative on every major league baseball team who speaks out against spit tobacco. And NSTEP's national chairman is Joe Garagiola, Hall of Fame broadcaster and former major league player.

McGowan says there has been progress. Only about 40 percent of major league ballplayers use spit tobacco. Many of them now chew bubblegum or sunflower seeds.

Ron Todd, director of tobacco control at the American Cancer Society, agrees spit tobacco doesn't seem to raise the same degree of alarm as cigarettes.

"I think [users] do recognize there are some health risks with it, but I think many of the users underestimate the risk," he says.

As well as being very addictive, spit tobacco causes cavities, periodontal disease, a precancerous condition called leukoplakia and cancer of the mouth, pharynx and throat, experts say.

## Regular Dental Exams Can Detect Problems

"Oral cancer is one of the most hideous cancers to treat and experience because you stand a good chance of losing part of the bone structure that supports your face, which makes it terribly disfiguring," Todd says.

He says regular dental exams can detect the effects of spit tobacco use.

"With spit tobacco, it is very easy for [people] to see the damage in the early stages before it gets too severe," Todd adds.

McGowan says spit tobacco users need to have a oral cancer–screening exam every time they visit their dentist.

*"There is considerable agreement in the scientific community that the use of smokeless tobacco involves significantly less risk of adverse health effects than cigarette smoking."*

# Smokeless Tobacco Use Is Less Harmful than Smoking

U.S. Smokeless Tobacco Company

The use of smokeless tobacco involves fewer health risks than smoking and therefore offers a viable alternative to cigarettes, the U.S. Smokeless Tobacco Company (USSTC) argues in the following viewpoint. It maintains that while smokeless tobacco is not entirely safe, using it is safer than smoking cigarettes. The tobacco company asserts that smokeless tobacco use by those who are unable to stop smoking cigarettes should be encouraged as a method of harm reduction. The U.S. Smokeless Tobacco Company is the leading producer of moist, smokeless tobacco and snuff in the United States.

As you read, consider the following questions:

1. According to the U.S. Smokeless Tobacco Company, why is a tobacco harm reduction strategy necessary?
2. According to a Royal College of Physicians report, how much less hazardous than smoking is the consumption of smokeless tobacco?
3. Which country has the highest rate of smokeless tobacco use and the lowest rate of cigarette smoking, according to the author?

U.S. Smokeless Tobacco Company, testimony before the House Committee on Energy and Commerce, Subcommittee on Commerce, Trade and Consumer Protection, Washington, D.C., June 3, 2003.

Since the Surgeon General's Report in 1964, there has been substantial public health discussion about the potential health effects of tobacco use. Various public health organizations have identified the risks of cigarette smoking as including cancer (*e.g.*, lung, oral cavity, esophagus, larynx, pancreas, bladder, kidney), chronic obstructive pulmonary disease, myocardial infarction, and stroke. The Centers for Disease Control and Prevention ("CDC") estimates that cigarette smoking caused approximately 442,000 premature deaths in the United States in 1999. The Surgeon General has indicated that the ideal way to avoid such health risks is to abstain from cigarette smoking. Nonetheless, 47 to 50 million adults in the U.S. continue to smoke cigarettes. This number represents approximately 25 percent of all U.S. adults.

The Surgeon General reached a judgment in 1986 that use of smokeless tobacco products "can cause cancer." Federally-mandated rotating warnings on smokeless tobacco product packaging and advertising state:

WARNING: THIS PRODUCT MAY CAUSE MOUTH CANCER

WARNING: THIS PRODUCT MAY CAUSE GUM DISEASE AND TOOTH LOSS

WARNING: THIS PRODUCT IS NOT A SAFE ALTERNATIVE TO CIGARETTES.

Numerous methods have been suggested by public health advocates for achieving tobacco harm reduction, including urging cigarette smokers to smoke fewer cigarettes, developing "less hazardous" cigarettes and creating alternative sources of nicotine, such as nicotine inhalers. A growing number of tobacco harm reduction proponents, however, are arguing for an additional method for achieving their goal. Based on the generally accepted view in the scientific community that smokeless tobacco use involves significantly less risk of adverse health effects than cigarette smoking, they would encourage those cigarette smokers who do not quit and do not use medicinal nicotine products to switch completely to smokeless tobacco products.

A logical starting point for discussion of smokeless tobacco in the context of tobacco harm reduction is the 600 page report issued in 2001 by the Institute of Medicine ("IOM") entitled: *Clearing the Smoke. Assessing the Science Base for Tobacco Harm Reduction* ("IOM Report"). The IOM was established in 1970 by the National Academy of Sciences to examine policy matters pertaining to public health, and acts under the Academy's congressional charter to be an advisor to the federal government and to assess issues relating to medical care, research and education. The IOM tobacco harm reduction project was undertaken at the request of, and was supported by, the U.S. Food and Drug Administration. The IOM Report explains the need for a tobacco harm reduction strategy as follows:

> Despite overwhelming evidence and widespread recognition that tobacco use poses a serious risk to health, some tobacco users cannot or will not quit. For those addicted tobacco users who do not quit, reducing the health risks of tobacco products themselves may be a sensible response. This is why many public health leaders believe that what has come to be called "harm reduction" must be included as a subsidiary component of a comprehensive public health policy toward tobacco.

Tobacco "harm reduction" is defined in the IOM Report as follows:

> *For the purposes of this report, a product is harm-reducing if it lowers total tobacco-related mortality and morbidity even though use of that product may involve continued exposure to tobacco related toxicants.* Many different policy strategies may contribute to harm reduction. However, this report focuses on tobacco products that may be less harmful or on pharmaceutical preparations that may be used alone or concomitantly with decreased use of conventional tobacco.

It is clear from this definition of "harm reduction" that, in the view of the IOM, it is not necessary to demonstrate that a product is "safe" or "harmless" in order for that product to play a role in tobacco harm reduction.

The IOM Report had the following to say with respect to smokeless tobacco products:

> Smokeless tobacco products are associated with oral cavity cancers, and a dose-response relationship exists. However, the overall risk is lower than for cigarette smoking, and some products such as Swedish snus [moist, ground tobacco used between the cheek and gum] may have no increased risk. It may be considered that such products could be used as a

PREP [Potential Reduced-Exposure Product] for persons addicted to nicotine, but these products must undergo testing as PREPs using the guidelines and research agenda contained herein. . . .

. . . The IOM Report's focus on the need for further research and demonstration of harm reduction benefits may be understandable in the context of new or novel tobacco products or so-called "safer" cigarettes. When it comes to smokeless tobacco, however, there is considerable agreement in the scientific community that the use of smokeless tobacco involves significantly less risk of adverse health effects than cigarette smoking. . . .

## Royal College of Physicians Report

In December 2002, the Royal College of Physicians [of London] ("RCP") issued a landmark report entitled *Protecting Smokers, Saving Lives*, which assessed various issues relating to future tobacco regulation in the United Kingdom. The RCP is England's oldest medical institution; among its main functions is to advise the government, the public and the medical profession on health care issues.

The 2002 RCP Report recognized that tobacco harm reduction must be an essential element of any tobacco regulation program:

A tobacco and nicotine regulatory authority should have a clear objective:

. . . to reduce the overall burden of tobacco-related disease by contributing to a reduction in smoking prevalence and by regulating to reduce the harm caused to continuing nicotine users.

The 2002 RCP Report also recognized that smokeless tobacco would be a key component of any tobacco harm reduction strategy:

Smokeless Tobacco:

As a way of using nicotine, the consumption of non-combustible tobacco is of the order of 10-1,000 times less hazardous than smoking, depending on the product. Some manufacturers want to market smokeless tobacco as a 'harm reduction' option for nicotine users, and they may find support for that in the public health community.

The issuance of the RCP's 2002 Report is not the first

time that the RCP has led the way on tobacco and health issues. In March 1962, the RCP issued a report on smoking and health which concluded that cigarette smoking caused lung cancer. Shortly after the issuance of that report, the U.S. Surgeon General, Dr. Luther L. Terry, established the Surgeon General's Advisory Committee on Smoking and Health to produce a similar report for the United States. That report was released in January 1964 and is generally referred to as the 1964 Surgeon General's Report. Its conclusions were similar to those of the 1962 RCP Report. . . .

## The Swedish Experience

Proponents of encouraging "inveterate" cigarette smokers to switch to smokeless tobacco products point to the history of cigarette smoking and smokeless tobacco use in Sweden as support for their view. Swedish males have the highest rate of smokeless tobacco use and the lowest rate of cigarette smoking of any Western country, and the daily use of smokeless tobacco by Swedish males now exceeds that of cigarettes (18.2 percent daily smokeless tobacco users versus 17.1 percent daily cigarette smokers). The following chart illustrates the changing pattern of tobacco use in Sweden during most of the past century, including the fact that smokeless tobacco use has overtaken cigarette smoking in

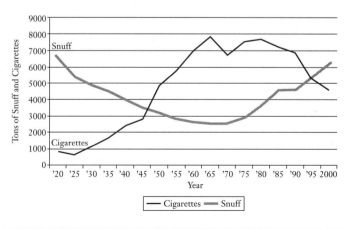

**Changing Pattern of Tobacco Use in Sweden**

recent years for the first time since World War II.

Tobacco and health researchers have linked Sweden's low rate of "tobacco-related mortality" to its high prevalence of smokeless tobacco use and low prevalence of cigarette smoking:

Sweden, with a long tradition of smokeless tobacco use (16% of adult males use smokeless tobacco daily) and the highest penetration of NRT [nicotine replacement therapy] use, is the only European country that has reached (19%) the World Health Organization's target of 20% smokers in the adult population by the year 2000; about 35% of all nicotine consumed comes from nonsmoked deliver[y] forms. The tobacco-related mortality in Sweden is by far lower than in any other European or North American country, although nicotine consumption may not be lower than in other countries.

In 2001, a *New Scientist* article summarized the Swedish experience in the context of tobacco harm reduction:

[S]mokers [in Sweden] aren't faced with the quit-or-die dilemma. Instead of using a nicotine replacement therapy with the aim of quitting both smoking and ultimately nicotine, they can continue using tobacco as a recreational drug, safe in the knowledge that it probably won't kill them. It's all down to a product called 'snus,' a form of moist ground tobacco that you pop between your lip and gum.

* * *

The 'Swedish experiment,' as it has come to be known, has inspired some health campaigners to press for a more enlightened approach to the smoking epidemic. It's a concept they call 'harm reduction.' 'If you look at Sweden, we have a living example of the concept in action,' says Clive Bates, director of ASH [Action on Smoking and Health].

# Periodical Bibliography

The following articles have been selected to supplement the diverse views presented in this chapter.

| | |
|---|---|
| *Alcoholism and Drug Abuse Weekly* | "Secondhand Smoke Poses Workplace Problems," September 25, 2000. |
| John Z. Ayanian and Paul D. Cleary | "Perceived Risks of Heart Disease and Cancer Among Cigarette Smokers," *Journal of the American Medical Association*, March 17, 1999. |
| Dave Barry | "Blowing Smoke," *Miami Herald*, October 24, 1999. |
| William F. Buckley | "What Are the Beleaguered Smokers to Do?" *Conservative Chronicle*, September 11, 2002. |
| John Elvin | "Individual Rights Going Up in Smoke," *Insight*, March 5, 2001. |
| *FCD Educational Services* | "Spit Tobacco: Just Say Ptooey," Winter 2000. www.fcd.org. |
| *Journal of School Health* | "Trends in Cigarette Smoking Among High School Students—United States, 1991–2001," August 2002. |
| Tom Majeski | "Teenage Smoking Drops 11% in 2 Years," *Pioneer Press*, September 20, 2002. www.twincities.com. |
| *Medical Letter on the CDC and FDA* | "Environmental Tobacco Smoke Exposure Associated with Respiratory Problems for Children," February 4, 2001. |
| Robert Preidt | "Chew on This: Experts Say Spit Tobacco Causes Gum Disease, Oral Cancer," *University of Maryland Medicine National Health News*, March 11, 2001. www.umm.edu. |
| Andy Rooney | "The Puff of Death," *Liberal Opinion Week*, December 13, 1999. |
| John Schwartz | "Reinventing the Cigarette," *Washington Post National Weekly Edition*, February 8, 1999. |
| Kathrine Stapp | "Smokeless Tobacco Industry Eyes New Market Niche," *Inter Press Service News Agency*, August 6, 2003. www.ipsnews.org. |
| Joan Stephenson | "A 'Safer' Cigarette? Prove It, Say Critics," *Journal of the American Medical Association*, May 17, 2000. |
| Elizabeth Whelan | "Mayor Bloomberg Exaggerates Secondhand Smoke Risk," *Health Facts and Fears*, December 12, 2002. www.healthfactsandfears.com. |
| Sidney Zion | "The Big Lie of Secondhand Smoke," *San Francisco Examiner*, November 29, 2002. |

# CHAPTER 2

# What Factors Contribute to Tobacco Use?

# Chapter Preface

Some teens start smoking because their friends smoke. Others begin because they think smoking will help them manage stress or lose weight. Recent research, however, indicates that over half—52.2 percent—of ten- to fourteen-year-olds who start smoking do so because they see actors smoking in movies. Further, the researchers maintain that seeing smoking in movies has a greater effect than traditional cigarette advertising and promotion on television or in magazine ads, which accounts for 34 percent of new experimentation with tobacco. In their study of over thirty-five hundred adolescents in Vermont and New Hampshire, scientists controlled for factors usually thought to have a strong effect on smoking initiation—friend, parent, or sibling smoking, rebelliousness, low self-esteem, receptivity to tobacco promotions, school performance, sensation-seeking propensity, parent education, authoritative parenting, and perception of parental disapproval of smoking. They concluded that none of these previously studied factors has as great an effect on teen tobacco use as seeing actors smoke in movies.

Moreover, the researchers found that the effect increases as teens watch more movies that show actors smoking. According to Madeline A. Dalton of Dartmouth Medical School, one of the designers of the study, "Our results suggest that viewing smoking in movies strongly predicts whether or not adolescents initiate smoking, and the effect increases significantly with greater exposure. Adolescents who viewed the most smoking in movies were almost three times more likely to initiate smoking than those with the least amount of exposure." Dalton and her colleagues maintain that their findings are important because exposure to movies that depict smoking is an almost universal teen experience. The researchers argue that reducing teen exposure to smoking in movies could help reduce the number of new teen smokers, many of whom will retain the habit throughout their lives.

Indeed, many in the tobacco control movement advocate giving an "adult content" or R rating to movies that depict smoking. Further, tobacco control advocates want a strong anti-smoking message run before films that portray smoking and closing credits attesting that no one associated with the movie received anything of value from tobacco companies. They also seek an end to cigarette brand identification within movies. Stanton A. Glantz, professor of medicine and director of the Center for Tobacco Control Research and Education at the University of California in San Francisco says, "The work by Dalton and colleagues, together with the earlier research in this area, strongly indicates that pushing for policy changes to reduce youth exposure to smoking in movies will have a rapid and substantial effect on youth smoking—and the subsequent disease and death smoking causes."

Watching actors smoke in movies contributes significantly to the likelihood that teens will start smoking. Authors in the following chapter debate many of the other factors that contribute to tobacco use in the United States.

| *"Most smokers use tobacco regularly because they are addicted to nicotine."*

# Nicotine Addiction Is the Major Cause of Tobacco Use

Christine H. Rowley

In the following viewpoint Christine H. Rowley argues that people use tobacco because they are addicted to nicotine. According to Rowley, nicotine is highly addictive and affects the brain in ways similar to cocaine and heroin. She maintains that cigarette smoking is the most efficient delivery system for nicotine and is thus the most prevalent form of nicotine addiction in the United States. However, cigars, pipes, and smokeless tobacco also provide powerful doses of nicotine. Rowley insists that cessation of nicotine use is typically accompanied by withdrawal symptoms, a further indication of the addictive properties of nicotine. Christine H. Rowley is a freelance editor and writer, desktop publisher, and Web page creator.

As you read, consider the following questions:
1. According to the author, when was nicotine first identified?
2. How many smokers try to quit each year, as cited by Rowley?
3. What chemical in the brain—thought to underlie pleasurable sensations—is released as an indirect result of nicotine use, according to the author?

Nicotine, one of more than 4,000 chemicals found in the smoke from tobacco products such as cigarettes, cigars, and pipes, is the primary component in tobacco that acts on the brain. Smokeless tobacco products such as snuff and chewing tobacco also contain many toxins as well as high levels of nicotine. Nicotine, recognized as one of the most frequently used addictive drugs, is a naturally occurring colorless liquid that turns brown when burned and acquires the odor of tobacco when exposed to air. There are many species of tobacco plants; the tabacum species serves as the major source of tobacco products today. Since nicotine was first identified in the early 1800s, it has been studied extensively and shown to have a number of complex and sometimes unpredictable effects on the brain and the body.

Cigarette smoking is the most prevalent form of nicotine addiction in the United States. Most cigarettes in the U.S. market today contain 10 milligrams (mg) or more of nicotine. Through inhaling smoke, the average smoker takes in 1 to 2 mg nicotine per cigarette. There have been substantial increases in the sale and consumption of smokeless tobacco products also, and more recently, in cigar sales.

Nicotine is absorbed through the skin and mucosal lining of the mouth and nose or by inhalation in the lungs. Depending on how tobacco is taken, nicotine can reach peak levels in the bloodstream and brain rapidly. Cigarette smoking, for example, results in rapid distribution of nicotine throughout the body, reaching the brain within 10 seconds of inhalation. Cigar and pipe smokers, on the other hand, typically do not inhale the smoke, so nicotine is absorbed more slowly through the mucosal membranes of their mouths. Nicotine from smokeless tobacco also is absorbed through the mucosal membranes.

## Is Nicotine Addictive?

Yes, nicotine is addictive. Most smokers use tobacco regularly because they are addicted to nicotine. Addiction is characterized by compulsive drug-seeking and use, even in the face of negative health consequences, and tobacco use certainly fits the description. It is well documented that most smokers identify tobacco as harmful and express a desire to reduce or stop using it, and nearly 35 million of them make a serious attempt to quit each year. Unfortunately, less than 7 percent of those who try to quit on their own achieve more than 1 year of abstinence; most relapse within a few days of attempting to quit.

Other factors to consider besides nicotine's addictive properties include its high level of availability, the small number of legal and social consequences of tobacco use, and the sophisticated marketing and advertising methods used by tobacco companies. These factors, combined with nicotine's addictive properties, often serve as determinants for first use and, ultimately, addiction.

Recent research has shown in fine detail how nicotine acts on the brain to produce a number of behavioral effects. Of primary importance to its addictive nature are findings that nicotine activates the brain circuitry that regulates feelings of pleasure, the so-called reward pathways. A key brain chemical involved in mediating the desire to consume drugs is the neurotransmitter dopamine, and research has shown that nicotine increases the levels of dopamine in the reward circuits. Nicotine's pharmacokinetic properties have been found also to enhance its abuse potential. Cigarette smoking produces a rapid distribution of nicotine to the brain, with drug levels peaking within 10 seconds of inhalation. The acute effects of nicotine dissipate in a few minutes, causing the smoker to continue dosing frequently throughout the day to maintain the drug's pleasurable effects and prevent withdrawal.

## Smoking Rushes Nicotine to the Brain

What people frequently do not realize is that *the cigarette is a very efficient and highly engineered drug-delivery system.* By inhaling, the smoker can get nicotine to the brain very rapidly with every puff. A typical smoker will take 10 puffs on a cigarette over a period of 5 minutes that the cigarette is lit. Thus, a person who smokes about 1½ packs (30 cigarettes) daily, gets 300 "hits" of nicotine to the brain each day. These factors contribute considerably to nicotine's highly addictive nature.

Scientific research is also beginning to show that nicotine may not be the only psychoactive ingredient in tobacco. Using advanced neuroimaging technology, scientists can see the dramatic effect of cigarette smoking on the brain and are finding a marked decrease in the levels of monoamineoxidase (MAO), an important enzyme that is responsible for breaking down dopamine. The change in MAO must be caused by some tobacco smoke ingredient other than nicotine, since we know that nicotine itself does not dramatically alter MAO levels. The decrease in two forms of MAO, A and B, then results in higher dopamine levels and may be another reason that smokers continue to smoke—to sustain the high dopamine levels that result in the desire for repeated drug use. . . .

## Nicotine's Effect Is Powerful

Nicotine can act as both a stimulant and a sedative. Immediately after exposure to nicotine, there is a "kick" caused in part by the drug's stimulation of the adrenal glands and resulting discharge of epinephrine (adrenaline). The rush of adrenaline stimulates the body and causes a sudden release of glucose as well as an increase in blood pressure, respiration, and heart rate. Nicotine also suppresses insulin output from the pancreas, which means that smokers are always slightly hyperglycemic. In addition, nicotine indirectly causes a release of dopamine in the brain regions that control pleasure and motivation. This reaction is similar to that seen with other drugs of abuse—such as cocaine and heroin—and it is thought to underlie the pleasurable sensations experienced by many smokers. In contrast, nicotine can also exert a sedative effect, depending on the level of the smoker's nervous system arousal and the dose of nicotine taken.

Chronic exposure to nicotine results in addiction. Research is just beginning to document all of the neurological changes that accompany the development and maintenance of nicotine addiction. The behavioral consequences of these changes are well documented, however. Greater than 90 percent of those smokers who try to quit without seeking treatment fail, with most relapsing within a week.

Repeated exposure to nicotine results in the development of tolerance, the condition in which higher doses of a drug are required to produce the same initial stimulation. Nicotine is metabolized fairly rapidly, disappearing from the body in a few hours. Therefore some tolerance is lost overnight, and smokers often report that the first cigarettes of the day are the strongest and/or the "best." As the day progresses, acute tolerance develops, and later cigarettes have less effect.

Cessation of nicotine use is followed by a withdrawal syndrome that may last a month or more; it includes symptoms that can quickly drive people back to tobacco use. Nicotine withdrawal symptoms include irritability, craving, cognitive and attentional deficits, sleep disturbances, and increased appetite and may begin within a few hours after the last cigarette. Symptoms peak within the first few days and may subside within a few weeks. For some people, however, symptoms may persist for months or longer.

An important but poorly understood component of the nicotine withdrawal syndrome is craving, an urge for nicotine that has been described as a major obstacle to successful abstinence. High levels of craving for tobacco may persist for 6 months or longer. While the withdrawal syndrome is related to the pharmacological effects of nicotine, many behavioral factors also can affect the severity of withdrawal symptoms. For some people, the feel, smell, and sight of a cigarette and the ritual of obtaining, handling, lighting, and smoking the cigarette are all associated with the pleasurable effects of smoking and can make withdrawal or craving worse. While nicotine gum and patches may alleviate the pharmacological aspects of withdrawal, cravings often persist.

*"Apart from numerous conceptual and definitional inadequacies, the notion that nicotine is an addictive substance lacks reasonable empirical support."*

# Nicotine Addiction Is Not the Major Cause of Tobacco Use

Dale M. Atrens

Dale M. Atrens contends in the following viewpoint that there is significant evidence contradicting the view that nicotine is addictive and little empirical evidence to support the claim. For example, nicotine does not produce any changes in the human brain usually associated with addictive drugs such as heroin and cocaine, he claims, proving that nicotine is not addicting. Atrens concludes that people use tobacco because doing so is pleasurable, not because they are addicted. Dale M. Atrens is a reader in psychobiology at the University of Sidney and the author of several neuroscience textbooks.

As you read, consider the following questions:
1. In Atrens's opinion what is wrong with a definition of addiction that might reasonably include nicotine?
2. What is the basis for the author's contention that nicotine lacks abuse potential?
3. Why does Atrens reject the notion that nicotine's withdrawal effects are proof of its abuse potential?

Dale M. Atrens, "Nicotine as an Addictive Substance: A Critical Examination of the Basic Concepts and Empirical Evidence," *Journal of Drug Issues*, June 2001.

The notion of nicotine addiction suffers from numerous and major conceptual, definitional, and empirical inadequacies. Some reflect general problems with the concept of addiction, whereas others are specific to nicotine.

A recurring source of difficulty for the nicotine addiction hypothesis is the continuing lack of consensus concerning a definition of addiction. Hundreds of definitions have been offered, yet none withstands any scrutiny. Rigorous definitions of addiction clearly exclude nicotine, whereas those that reasonably include nicotine also include so many other substances and events that the notion of addiction becomes trivialized.

Lacking a reasonable definition of addiction, the putative addictiveness of drugs has become a matter of legislative fiat, judicial rulings, and committee edicts. Not surprisingly, which drugs are considered addictive varies markedly over time and in different places. Cannabis was long considered to be the scourge of our youth while tobacco was considered relatively harmless. Recently this position has been reversed. This is not science, but politics.

Self-administration studies in laboratory species are said to support the view that nicotine, much like heroin and cocaine, is powerfully reinforcing. However, nicotine self-administration doesn't remotely approach the vigor or reliability of that supported by drugs such as cocaine and heroin. The strongest reinforcing effects of nicotine in laboratory species are less than those of innocuous reinforcers such as light, sound, sugar, or salt.

## Only Humans Like Nicotine

Moreover, nicotine self-administration requires doses that are far higher than humans ever encounter. These effects may well represent monoaminergic effects of high nicotine doses. There are no reports of nicotine self-administration in laboratory species at doses even approaching those self-administered by humans. It is unjustified to use weak and inconsistent reinforcement effects obtained with high intravenous doses in laboratory species as evidence for human abuse potential.

Perhaps the most serious deficiency in using animal models to study human drug taking is that animals do not seem to get 'hooked' on any substance. This is particularly true of nicotine. It is difficult to show any rewarding effects of nicotine in laboratory species, let alone the powerful effects associated with drugs of abuse. It is possible that drug abuse is a uniquely human phenomenon.

Like the data from animal experimentation, the data on nicotine reinforcement in humans do not suggest that nicotine has abuse potential. There are no credible demonstrations in humans that nicotine is any more reinforcing than many other substances and events that have no abuse potential. The subjective effects of nicotine suggest a drug that is pleasant, nothing more. In this crucial respect, nicotine contrasts markedly with reference drugs such as cocaine and heroin that consistently produce strong feelings of euphoria.

---

## Nicotine Is Not Addictive

Professor John Davis (University of Strathclyde) put things in perspective when he said, 'What I don't agree with is the idea that people who use nicotine become . . . helpless addicts who have no say in the choice of this activity—that the nicotine compels them to smoke. The evidence is simply not there. People give up smoking all the time . . . '

Freedom Organization for the Right to Enjoy Smoking Tobacco (FOREST) Online, June 1, 2003. www.forestonline.org.

---

There have been attempts to lend credibility to the notion of addiction by describing it as a brain disease. However, there is little evidence for such a view. There is no special brain state associated with nicotine use. Although nicotine has diverse effects on the brain, none has any significant potential to perpetuate nicotine use. Moreover, the neural effects of nicotine and other putatively addictive drugs are indistinguishable from those produced by many relatively harmless substances and everyday experiences.

Nicotine has effects on dopaminergic transmission that, in certain respects, resemble those of cocaine or heroin. However, almost anything that alters arousal alters dopaminergic transmission. Such neurochemical effects should not be interpreted as a correlate of addiction. The fact that some of the effects on dopamine transmission may be restricted to the shell of the nucleus accumbens is interesting, but irrelevant to whether nicotine or anything else is addictive.

## Dopamine Involvement Is Not Conclusive

The finding that dopamine may be involved in the effects of nicotine and reinforcement processes lends no support to the notion that nicotine is addictive. The dopamine hypothesis of reinforcement remains an intensely debated issue in which the theory, methodology, and empirical findings are all disputed. Claims to the contrary notwithstanding, none of the many variants of the dopamine theory has, as yet, any implications for human drug use. There is no justification for making the major leap from the poorly understood neural sequelae of reinforcement in laboratory species to the still more poorly defined and understood notion of addiction in humans.

The effects of nicotine, like those of virtually every other drug, psychoactive or not, show a degree of tolerance. It is questionable whether this ubiquitous phenomenon says anything about abuse potential. It certainly does not distinguish nicotine from many other innocuous substances.

Nicotine use may sometimes produce withdrawal effects. However, many drugs with no abuse potential produce withdrawal effects that are much more dramatic than those produced by nicotine. Conversely, many drugs with substantial abuse potential produce little in the way of withdrawal effects. Additionally, nicotine withdrawal effects last for no more than a few weeks, whereas relapse potential may last for years. The fact that withdrawal and relapse potential have such different temporal characteristics indicates that they cannot be causally related.

In summary, apart from numerous conceptual and definitional inadequacies, the notion that nicotine is an addictive substance lacks reasonable empirical support. There are so many and such grossly conflicting findings that adhering to the nicotine addiction thesis is only defensible on political, not scientific, grounds. More broadly, addiction may have some use as a description of certain types of behavior, but it fails badly as an explanation of such behaviors.

It is commonly assumed that questioning the addiction hypothesis is to condone and even advocate drug use. Such an assumption is incorrect. In order to develop effective treatments for drug problems, it is necessary to escape from the unproductive ideology that is currently dominant. Abandoning the concept of addiction is a step in this direction.

> *"Relatively few people start smoking or switch brands after age 18. So tobacco companies developed ad campaigns to lure teens."*

# Tobacco Advertising Encourages Teens to Smoke

Kathiann M. Kowalski

Tobacco companies target their advertising to teens because they want to replace older smokers who die from tobacco-related diseases, argues Kathiann M. Kowalski in the following viewpoint. She contends that the four major tobacco companies have not kept their 1998 promise to stop marketing their products to youth. Tobacco companies continue to target teens by advertising in magazines with a significant teen readership, she asserts. Kowalski maintains that teens must resist the tobacco companies' efforts to manipulate them into becoming smokers. Kathiann M. Kowalski writes nonfiction books, stories, and articles for teens and young adults.

As you read, consider the following questions:
1. In Kowalski's opinion, how do tobacco companies try to lure teens into becoming smokers?
2. According to the author, how many teens are reached by tobacco advertising?
3. To what does Kowalski attribute the recent drop in teen smoking?

Kathiann M. Kowalski, "How Tobacco Ads Target Teens," *Current Health 2*, vol. 28, April/May 2002, pp. 6–7. Copyright © 2002 by Weekly Reader Corp. Reproduced by permission.

"**N**o Boundaries. No Bull," reads the full-page cigarette ad in a recent issue of *Rolling Stone*. The tobacco company and its ad agency would say the rebellious tone of the in-your-face ad is not aimed at teens. But the magazine sits on the shelves of an Ohio public library's young adult/teen section. And the same issue carries a full-page ad for candy.

Coincidence? Probably not.

Crafty marketing? Almost certainly.

## The Hook

For decades, tobacco companies have focused marketing efforts on teens. Why? Because companies want to replace older smokers who die from tobacco-related illnesses. As a 1981 Philip Morris document said, "Today's teenager is tomorrow's potential regular customer, and the overwhelming majority of smokers first begin to smoke while in their teens."

Relatively few people start smoking or switch brands after age 18. So tobacco companies developed ad campaigns to lure teens. Themes included rugged independence, freedom, popularity, individuality, social acceptance, and carefree fun. Giveaways and promotional products became popular too. All these youth-appealing themes are still prominent in tobacco marketing.

In 1998, 46 states and the four major tobacco companies agreed to settle lawsuits for billions of dollars in tobacco-related health costs. The tobacco companies promised they would not "take any action, directly or indirectly, to target youth . . . in the advertising, promotion, or marketing of tobacco products."

The very next year, however, the money tobacco companies spent on magazine ads shot up 33 percent to $291.1 million. Sixty percent of that went for ads in youth-oriented magazines. Those magazines have at least 15 percent or 2 million readers ages 12 to 17. In 2000, magazine ad spending dropped back near presettlement levels to $216.9 million. Spending for youth-oriented magazine ads was still 59 percent. Tobacco ads in adult magazines such as *Time* reach many teens too. The Centers for Disease Control and Prevention (CDC) estimates that tobacco advertising reaches more than 80 percent of teens.

"They're being heavily targeted by the industry," says Dr. Michael Siegel at Boston University's School of Public Health. "They need to resist and rebel against the tobacco industry's attempt to recruit them as essentially lifelong customers."

Dr. Siegel and his colleagues have documented tobacco marketing's success with teens. With cigarettes costing $3 or more per pack, price should play a big role in consumer choices. But the most popular brands among teens are the ones most heavily advertised.

Similarly, African-American teens tend to use the menthol brands advertised most in ethnically oriented magazines. "It's hard to explain the brand preferences of African-American youth on the basis of any factor other than advertising," notes Dr. Siegel.

Even "anti-smoking" ads sponsored by the industry can give the opposite message. Some ads funded by tobacco companies stress how conscientious storeowners don't sell tobacco to underage buyers. An implicit message is that smoking is a "grown-up" thing. However, three-fourths of adults don't smoke. Likewise, ads about good works by "the people at" a large tobacco company ignore the disease, pain, and suffering caused by their products.

In Logan, Utah, a tobacco company gave away book covers that said, "Think. Don't Smoke." But, the word "don't" was a different color, notes 18-year-old Marin Poole, "So THINK SMOKE stood out." One design featured an angry snowboarder. "The snowboard looked like a lit match, and the clouds looked more like smoke than clouds," Marin says. Her campaign to get the book covers out of Logan High School, plus other anti-smoking efforts, earned her the Campaign for Tobacco-Free Kids' 2001 Youth Advocate of the Year award for the western region.

Cynthia Loesch won the award for the eastern region. In 1998, her group persuaded a major Boston newspaper to stop accepting tobacco ads. Cynthia continues to educate people—both adults and youth—about tobacco. "It's a fact that cigarettes do absolutely nothing for you, and all they lead to is illnesses and eventually death," says Cynthia.

# Starstruck

Stars smoking in films or off-screen include Leonardo Di Caprio, Neve Campbell, Sylvester Stallone, Gillian Anderson, Ashley Judd, Sean Penn, John Travolta, and more. In a recent Dartmouth University study, young people were 16 times more likely to use tobacco if their favorite actor did. In another Dartmouth study, middle school students allowed to watch R-rated films (more inclined to show smoking and drinking) were five times more likely to try cigarettes and alcohol than those whose parents wouldn't let them watch R-rated films.

Even G, PG, and PG-13 movies often show tobacco use. In *The Muppet Movie*, for example, three cigar-smoking humans interacted with the Muppets.

"When movie stars are smoking in their movies or in front of young people, they're almost just as responsible as the tobacco industry is for addicting young people," maintains 17-year-old Shannon Brewer, the 2001 National Youth Advocate of the Year for the Campaign for Tobacco-Free Kids. "Whether or not they use it all the time, it's an influence on kids because it's saying that's what it takes in order to be that star."

Of course, not all actors smoke—and some take a stand against tobacco and other drugs. Actor Jeremy London, model Christy Turlington, and various other celebrities, for example, work with the CDC, American Lung Association, or Campaign for Tobacco-Free Kids to present positive role models.

Yet too many moviemakers use cigarettes and cigars as quick cliche props. "If they're creative producers and directors, they should be able to portray attractive characters through other means," challenges Dr. Siegel.

## The Number One Killer

Very few legal products are deadly when used as directed. Tobacco, however, is America's No. 1 killer. According to the CDC, 430,000 Americans die each year from tobacco-related causes. Inhaled smoke and chewed tobacco directly affect the user. Secondhand smoke affects people who live, work, or socialize with smokers.

Nicotine is tobacco's addictive "hook." At least 63 of the other 4,000 chemicals in tobacco cause cancer, according to the American Lung Association. The list of toxic ingredients also includes tar, carbon monoxide, arsenic, hydrogen cyanide, acetylene, benzene, and formaldehyde. Lung cancer and cancers of the stomach, pancreas, mouth, throat, and esophagus are all linked to tobacco. Tobacco also kills by causing heart attacks, strokes, and other circulatory diseases.

Besides direct deaths, tobacco makes people more susceptible to bronchitis, pneumonia, asthma, and other illnesses. Tobacco reduces lung capacity and impairs an athlete's performance. Smoking during pregnancy increases risks of miscarriage, premature birth, and sudden infant death syndrome (SIDS).

## Cigarette Ads Target Youth

Despite an explicit ban on directing cigarette advertising at children, all three major U.S. tobacco companies selectively increased youth targeting after the prohibition was put in place in 1998 report researchers from the University of Chicago in the March/April [2002] issue of *Health Affairs*. . . .

"What we found was a violation of the spirit and the letter of the 1998 settlement," said Paul Chung, M.D., a Robert Wood Johnson Clinical Scholar at the University of Chicago and co-first author of the paper. "Cigarette companies had to become slightly more subtle about it, but they continue to aim their advertising at people under 18."

John Easton, University of Chicago Hospitals, March 12, 2002.

Tobacco messes with your mind too. Some teen smokers say smoking relaxes them. But researcher Andy Parrott at the University of East London found that teen smokers' stress levels increased as regular smoking patterns developed. Any perceived relaxation was just temporary relief of nicotine withdrawal between cigarettes. In short, cigarette smoking caused stress.

In another study reported by the American Academy of Pediatrics, teen smokers were nearly four times as likely as nonsmokers to develop serious symptoms of depression. Depression is a mental illness that hampers day-to-day functioning. Severe cases can even lead to suicide.

Beyond this, tobacco stains teeth and nails. It dulls skin and hair. Smoke reeks and lingers on hair and clothing. Instead of making people attractive, smoking does just the opposite.

## Nasty Nicotine

About 60 percent of current teen smokers have tried to quit within the past year, reports the CDC. Most started out thinking they could quit at any time. But nicotine addiction seizes control before teens realize they're hooked—sometimes within days or weeks after the first cigarette.

Pure nicotine is deadly. Tobacco, however, delivers just enough nicotine (1 to 2 mg in the average cigarette) to hook users. You might say that cigarettes are engineered as highly effective drug delivery devices.

The National Institute on Drug Abuse reports that nicotine increases dopamine levels in the brain's "reward circuits" within 10 seconds of inhaling. The neurotransmitter dopamine increases feelings of pleasure. Nicotine also decreases the brain's levels of monoamine oxidase (MAO), an enzyme that breaks down excess dopamine.

Nicotine's peak effects dissipate within minutes. Users then need more nicotine to sustain the feeling. So, they smoke more. Depending on a person's arousal state, nicotine can be both a stimulant and a sedative.

When addicted users don't get nicotine, they experience withdrawal. Symptoms include cravings, anxiety, nervousness, and irritability. Thanks to nicotine, the tobacco industry often hooks customers for life.

## Knowledge Is Power

Media messages that show tobacco favorably entice teens to smoke. But anti-smoking advertising can counter those influences. Dr. Siegel and his colleagues found that teens who regularly receive anti-smoking messages are twice as likely not to smoke as teens who don't get that exposure.

Instead of thinking that "everybody" smokes, teens were more likely to believe that only about one-fourth of American adults and teens smoke—which is true. In other words, getting the facts about smoking helps teens tell the difference between tobacco companies' media myths and reality, notes Dr. Siegel.

In fact, researchers at the University of Michigan found that from 1996 to 2001 the percentage of eighth graders who were smoking dropped to 12 percent from 21 percent; tenth graders who were smoking fell to 21 percent, down from 30 percent. Among 12th graders, the number of smokers dropped to 30 percent in 2001, down from a 37 percent peak in 1997. This drop in teen smoking is attributed to anti-smoking campaigns.

Anti-smoking ordinances and restaurant bans help too. Such rules reduce bystanders' exposure to secondhand smoke. Plus, they keep people from being constantly assaulted by tobacco's pervasive odor. "In towns that don't allow smoking in restaurants," notes Dr. Siegel, "kids are more likely to perceive that fewer people in their community smoke. They're not constantly smelling it and being exposed to it."

The more you know about tobacco and its consequences, the better prepared you'll be to resist media influences and peer pressure to smoke. Practice saying "No, thanks," or "I don't want to," in case a friend offers you tobacco. Better yet, say "I'd prefer if you didn't smoke around me. The smoke really bothers me." Real friends respect each other's wishes.

Whether you're 16 or 60, tobacco takes a toll on health. Encourage everyone around you to avoid tobacco. And be smart. Don't let the tobacco industry trap you.

*"Cigarette ads are not the problem. . . . Kids smoke because of peer pressure, because their parents smoke and because they are rebelling against authority."*

# Tobacco Advertising Is Not Responsible for Teen Smoking

Robert A. Levy

In the following viewpoint Robert A. Levy claims that tobacco companies are not specifically targeting teens when they advertise in general interest magazines. Levy argues further that tobacco ads are not responsible for teen smoking. He contends that teens begin to smoke for many reasons, including peer pressure and a desire to rebel, and tobacco companies should not be wrongly blamed for teens' tobacco habits. Robert A. Levy is senior fellow in constitutional studies at the Cato Institute.

As you read, consider the following questions:
1. According to Levy, why was Philip Morris eager to curtail its magazine advertising?
2. What was the result of a five-year Justice Department investigation of tobacco companies, in the author's opinion?
3. What does Levy argue is the purpose of cigarette ads?

E xuding self-righteousness, California [attorney general] Bill Lockyer has pounced on tobacco companies for running cigarette ads in magazines like *People*, *Sports Illustrated* and *TV Guide*. Lockyer's fulmination, triggered by the release of a study in *The New England Journal of Medicine*, came in the wake of his lawsuit against [tobacco company] R.J. Reynolds for having "continuously and systematically targeted youth" by advertising in magazines with substantial teen readership.

The attorney general didn't find it necessary to inform Californians that the study was partly funded by a public official now suing a tobacco company. Nor did Lockyer mention that the study's co-author is a long-time activist and former board member of California's rabidly anti-tobacco clique, Americans for Nonsmokers' Rights.

It seems that Lockyer's search for hobgoblins has its limits. Yes, he has assailed the hapless tobacco industry. And he engaged in some light-hearted banter when he suggested that Enron Corp. Chairman Kenneth Lay, who has never been charged with an illegal act, is nonetheless responsible for California's energy problems and should, therefore, be put in "an 8-by-10 cell" so he could be exposed to prison rape.

Yet Californians haven't heard a peep from their attorney general on media violence, even though Sen. Joseph Lieberman, D-Conn., proclaimed that entertainment companies peddling adult material to children is "not a partisan issue." Evidently, Lockyer's professed concern for teen-agers is put under wraps when his Hollywood pals denounce legislation that might impose financial penalties on moviemakers.

On the tobacco front, Lockyer complains that the multistate settlement agreement proscribes cigarette ads in magazines read by lots of kids. In fact, the settlement only commits the industry not to target underage smokers.

## Tobacco Companies Curtailed Their Ads

That amorphous provision—in stark contrast to specific bans in the settlement on billboards and bus ads—has been interpreted differently by the several companies. Philip Morris, the market leader, with a vested interest in securing its dominance by restricting competitive advertising, has been almost eager to rein in its magazine ads. The three other tobacco giants also curtailed their ads, but not as aggressively as Philip Morris.

Still, all four companies have surpassed the standard laid down by the Federal Trade Commission, which negotiated a voluntary ban on liquor ads in magazines with more than 30 percent of its readership below the legal drinking age. The FTC, by the way, claims that, "This practice . . . minimizes the number of underage consumers reached by alcohol advertising without unduly interfering with the advertiser's ability to reach a legal-age audience."

## Ads Do Not Make Teens Smoke

In 1988, R.J. Reynolds introduced its Joe Camel cartoon icon designed to market Camel cigarettes. Everyone from Ralph Nader and anti-tobacco groups to the Centers for Disease Control to conservative tobacco-state lawmakers insisted cigarette ads, especially Joe Camel, lure teens to smoke. Yet, none mentioned the startling fact that in the four years after Joe's advent, every survey showed teenage smoking declined—down 19 percent among high schoolers from 1988 to 1992, twice as fast as the drop among adults.

Further, the biggest decline came among the youngest group (12–13). It wasn't until 1993, when cigarette ad spending fell and market analysts agreed Joe Camel was old hat, that teenage smoking went up.

Surprisingly, over the last 25 years, teen smoking and smoking initiation rates are negatively associated with cigarette advertising and promotion spending—that is, the more companies spend, the less teens smoke, and vice-versa.

Mike Males, AlterNet, May 22, 2001.

That doesn't impress Lockyer. Neither do the results of a five-year Justice Department investigation that was unable to produce a single indictment of a tobacco executive for marketing to minors, despite painstaking efforts by prosecutors and FBI agents, testimony by whistle-blowers, and disgorgement of millions of new documents.

None of that matters. Rather than more vigorous enforcement of California laws that foreclose the sale of cigarettes to minors, Lockyer has decided that kids will become more responsible if they don't see magazine ads—even if they do see their state's chief law enforcement officer flout the First Amendment in pursuit of his anti-tobacco crusade. Our constitution protects Klan speech, flag burning and gangsta rap (targeted directly at teen-agers). But if R.J. Reynolds advertises Camel cigarettes in *Sports Illustrated*, which is read overwhelmingly by adults, the boot of Lockyer's state government will come down hard on the company's neck.

In the commercial speech context, the Supreme Court has laid down some important principles: A 1983 opinion held that adult discourse cannot be confined to conversations you might hear in a sandbox. Government must not "reduce the adult population—to reading only what is fit for children." And 13 years later, the court affirmed that even "vice" products like alcoholic beverages are entitled to commercial speech protection.

That was followed, this most recent term, by *Lorillard vs. Reilly*, in which the court threw out Massachusetts regulations that banned tobacco billboards within 1,000 feet of a school and required retail store ads to be five feet off the floor if kids under 18 were admitted. Clearly, the Supreme Court is not willing to validate regulations that sweep too broadly. Lockyer needs to read the cases.

Cigarette ads are not the problem. Like automobile ads, they are designed to encourage brand shifting. Indeed, six European countries that have prohibited tobacco ads found that teen consumption increased. Kids smoke because of peer pressure, because their parents smoke and because they are rebelling against authority. Those are the problems that have to be addressed, without violating commercial speech rights and without preventing adults from looking at magazine advertisements.

*"Researchers found that among the 3,356 twin pairs studied, genetic factors make a stronger contribution to nicotine dependence (61 percent) than do environmental factors (39 percent)."*

# Genetics Plays a Role in Tobacco Use

Patrick Zickler

A person's vulnerability to nicotine addiction may be determined in part by his or her genetic makeup, Patrick Zickler contends in the following viewpoint. He argues that National Institute on Drug Abuse (NIDA)-supported studies conducted on twins show that genetic factors play a much more significant role than environmental factors in determining nicotine dependence. He maintains that a more complete understanding of the role of genetic influences in nicotine addiction will help scientists develop better treatments to help people stop smoking. Patrick Zickler is a staff writer for *NIDA Notes.*

As you read, consider the following questions:

1. According to Zickler, why do researchers use twins to determine whether genes play a role in nicotine addiction?
2. What purpose does Zickler maintain is served by genes that help regulate nicotine metabolism?
3. In the author's opinion, why might anxious people smoke more and have more difficulty quitting?

Patrick Zickler, "Evidence Builds That Genes Influence Cigarette Smoking," *NIDA Notes*, vol. 15, August 2000.

More than one in four Americans older than 17 regularly smokes cigarettes despite increasing public awareness of tobacco's severe health risks. Some start younger than others and, among those who try to quit, some are more successful than others. NIDA [National Institute on Drug Abuse]-supported scientists are finding increasing evidence that these differences may be due in part to an inherited vulnerability to nicotine addiction.

At the St. Louis University Health Sciences Center, Dr. William True and Dr. Hong Xian interviewed male twin pairs to assess genetic influences on smoking. In twin studies, researchers compare patterns of tobacco use in fraternal and identical twin pairs, who typically are exposed to common environmental influences. If genes play a role in determining tobacco use, identical twins—who share the same genes—will be more similar in their use of tobacco than fraternal twins, who share roughly half of their genes. The St. Louis University researchers found that among the 3,356 twin pairs studied, genetic factors make a stronger contribution to nicotine dependence (61 percent) than do environmental factors (39 percent) and also play a more prominent role (55 percent) than environmental factors (45 percent) in alcohol dependence. In another study, Dr. Kenneth Kendler and his colleagues at the Medical College of Virginia in Richmond interviewed 949 female twin pairs and found that genetic factors play a more important role (78 percent) than do environmental factors (22 percent) in smoking initiation and in nicotine dependence (72 percent vs. 28 percent).

## Understanding Genetic Influences

"These studies emphasize the importance of understanding the role of genetic influences in smoking," says Dr. Jaylan Turkkan, chief of NIDA's Behavioral Sciences Research Branch. "The more we understand about vulnerabilities, risks, and possible protective factors, the better able we will be to tailor treatments that help people stop smoking."

Other NIDA-supported scientists are studying genes that are polymorphic—that is, in different individuals the same gene has slight variations called alleles—and have found that individuals with one type of allele are more likely to begin smoking or to have greater success quitting than are individuals with another type. For example, researchers at the University of Toronto have found that different alleles in a gene that helps regulate nicotine metabolism may protect some smokers from becoming dependent on nicotine.

## Genetic vs. Environmental Influences on Smoking and Drinking

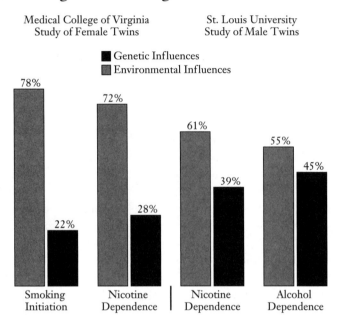

*A Medical College of Virginia study involving 949 female twin pairs found genetic factors to be more influential than environmental factors in smoking initiation and nicotine dependence. Likewise, a St. Louis University study of 3,356 male twin pairs found genetic factors to be more influential for dependence on nicotine and alcohol.*

NIDA Notes, August 2000.

Dr. Caryn Lerman, principal investigator of the NIDA-supported Transdisciplinary Tobacco Use Research Center at Georgetown University in Washington, D.C., and her colleagues studied two genes, designated SLC6A3 and DRD2, that may influence smoking behavior by affecting the action of the brain chemical dopamine. In a study involving 289 smokers and 233 nonsmokers (42 percent male, 58 percent female, average age 43), the researchers found that smokers were less likely to have an allele designated SLC6A3-9 (46.7 percent) than were nonsmokers (55.8 percent). The likelihood of smoking was even lower if the individual had both the SLC6A3-9 allele and the DRD2-A2 allele. In addition, Dr. Lerman observed that smokers with the SLC6A3-9 allele were more likely to have started smoking later and to have had longer periods of smoking cessation than those without the allele. These findings imply that the allele may impart a protective effect. Therefore, Dr. Lerman suggests, smokers without the SLC6A3-9 allele may be better able to quit smoking if their treatment incorporates a medication such as bupropion that acts on the brain's dopamine pathway. This hypothesis is currently being tested in a randomized trial.

## Developing New Treatments

Dr. Lerman and her colleagues also studied a polymorphism in a gene, designated 5-HTTLPR, that helps regulate the brain chemical serotonin to determine the gene's possible role in smoking. The polymorphism has two alleles, one designated the short, or S, allele, the other the long, or L allele. In previous studies the S allele has been linked to neuroticism—an anxiety-related personality trait. Dr. Lerman and her colleagues studied 185 smokers (46 percent male, 54 percent female, and average age 45) to investigate the possible relationship between genetically influenced neuroticism and smoking behavior. They found that neuroticism was associated with increased nicotine dependence, smoking for stimulation, and smoking to relieve negative mood in the group of smokers who had the S allele. Among smokers with the L allele, neuroticism was not associated with these smoking patterns. "Anxious persons tend to smoke more and have more difficulty quitting," Dr. Lerman says. The new findings suggest that among smokers with neuroticism, determining the 5-HTTLPR genotype may help identify who will be more responsive to a particular type of treatment. "Once validated, these results may lead to targeted pharmacotherapy for smoking cessation," says Dr. Lerman.

"This area of research represents our first small steps along a very complicated path to understanding the role that genes play in drug abuse," notes Dr. Harold Gordon of NIDA's Clinical Neurobiology Branch. "Many genes interact with each other and with other biological and environmental factors. Defining these interactions and understanding their influence on nicotine addiction will be crucial to development of treatments for smoking and for other addictions."

# Periodical Bibliography

The following articles have been selected to supplement the diverse views presented in this chapter.

B. Bower — "Youthful Nicotine Addiction May Be Growing," *Science News*, September 22, 2001.

John Easton — "Cigarette Ads Target Youth, Violating $250 Billion 1998 Settlement," *University of Chicago Hospitals Press Release*, March 12, 2002.

Michael Eisner et al. — "And the Losers Are . . ." *Daily Variety*, March 24, 2003.

50PlusHealth — "Addiction: Is It in Our Genes?" January 29, 2003. www.50plushealth.co.uk.

Michael Fitzpatrick — "Addiction Addicts," *Spiked Online*, March 13, 2001. www.spiked-online.com.

Mignon Fogarty — "Depending on Cigarettes, Counting on Science," *Scientist*, March 24, 2003.

Health and Medicine Week — "Anger and Anxiety May Trigger Urge to Smoke in Some People," September 10, 2001.

Health and Medicine Week — "Movie Smoking Linked to Teens Trying First Cigarette," January 7, 2002.

Elizabeth Kassab — "'U' Prof. Explores Nicotine, Gene Relationship," *Michigan Daily*, September 15, 2000. www.michigandaily.com.

Susan J. Landers — "Anti-Tobacco Activists Lift Smokescreen Behind Teen Smoking," *American Medical News*, April 1, 2002.

David N. Leff — "*Science Scan* Jury Still Far Out on Controversial Benefit of Smoking to Alzheimer's Disease, Scripps Chemists Report," *Bioworld Today*, June 16, 2003.

Pat MacDonald — "Nicotine Addiction," *Practice Nurse*, November 8, 2002.

Ted Roberts — "I Never Dream of Nicotine," *Ideas on Liberty*, May 2003.

Gilbert L. Ross — "What Physicians Don't Know About Smoking," *Priorities for Health*, 2001.

Sat Sharma and Morley Lertzmaan — "Nicotine Addiction," *E-Medicine*, January 21, 2003. www.emedicine.com.

Elisabeth Simantov — "Health-Compromising Behaviors: Why Do Adolescents Smoke or Drink?" *Journal of the American Medical Association*, January 24, 2001.

# CHAPTER 3

# How Can Tobacco Use Be Reduced?

# Chapter Preface

Two out of every three smokers in the United States try to quit. Some stop smoking abruptly—"cold turkey"—and suffer the unpleasant effects of nicotine withdrawal. Others choose nicotine replacement therapy in the form of a patch, gum, lozenge, or inhaler, attempting to wean themselves gradually from their nicotine addiction. Many combine pharmaceutical therapy with antismoking counseling. Unfortunately, few smokers—less than 3 percent—quit permanently. However, according to a research report in *Lancet*, an injectable nicotine vaccine will soon be available, and it could mean the end to nicotine addiction for even the heaviest smokers. Scientists at pharmaceutical companies in the United States and Great Britain have been working on a nicotine vaccine since the late 1990s, and several began clinical trials on human volunteers in 2001 and 2002. The new nicotine vaccine could reduce tobacco use by helping current smokers quit and, some scientists argue, discouraging teen tobacco experimenters from taking up the habit. According to Clive Bates, director of London's Action on Smoking and Health, "A nicotine vaccine would be a profound development, which would effectively become one of the most important medicines in the response to cancer, lung and heart disease."

The nicotine vaccine under development stimulates the body's immune system to recognize and destroy an invading organism—the nicotine molecule. The immune system binds every nicotine molecule in the smoker's blood and destroys it before it reaches the brain. Because little or no nicotine passes from the blood to the brain, the smoker does not feel the rewarding—and addictive—effect of the nicotine. Without the reinforcement of a nicotine reward, smokers who are trying to quit are less likely to "slip" and start using tobacco again. David Gury, manufacturer of NicVAX, one of the nicotine vaccines being tested in the United States, maintains, "You don't get that feel-goodness that nicotine provides you when it gets into the brain. So if you stop that process, it should help you stop smoking."

While most researchers are confident that a nicotine vaccine will help smokers quit, some are less sure about the efficacy of such a drug as a preventative measure, especially for adolescents. Wayne Hall writes in *Lancet*, "Public experience of vaccines against infectious diseases may raise the expectation that a nicotine vaccine will provide almost complete protection against smoking for life." He cautions parents who want to vaccinate their youngsters against smoking that vaccines currently being tested are of limited duration and would require periodic booster shots to maintain protection. Further, he argues that a guarantee of the long-term safety of nicotine vaccines is years away. Hall insists, "Any trials of preventative use of a nicotine vaccine in adolescents should probably only be done, if at all, after extensive experience in use of the vaccine with adult smokers."

The new nicotine vaccine promises to be a valuable smoking cessation aid. Authors in the following chapter explore the effectiveness of other measures aimed at reducing tobacco use.

*"Agreement is fairly widespread, including among some in the tobacco industry itself, on the fundamental elements that should go into FDA regulation of tobacco products."*

# The Food and Drug Administration Should Regulate Tobacco Products

David A. Kessler

In the following viewpoint David A. Kessler argues that because nicotine is a drug, the Food and Drug Administration (FDA), which regulates all legal addictive drugs, should regulate tobacco products. Further, he maintains that FDA regulation of tobacco should aim to limit marketing to youth and work toward removing harmful ingredients from tobacco products. Adequate funding for smoking-cessation research and the development of safer cigarettes should also be part of FDA guidelines, he contends. David A. Kessler, former commissioner of the FDA, is dean of Yale Medical School.

As you read, consider the following questions:

1. According to Kessler, what was the only part of the tobacco legislation before Congress that was not challenged?
2. What does the Supreme Court fear the FDA would do to cigarettes if the agency was allowed to regulate tobacco, in the author's opinion?
3. What has the FDA's effort regarding cigarettes thus far accomplished, in Kessler's view?

The Supreme Court—no matter how noble and correct its words about the public health threat posed by cigarettes—got it fundamentally wrong in denying the Food and Drug Administration (FDA) the ability to regulate tobacco products.

But the court's decision [in March 2000] gives the sense that all nine justices would like to see the agency deal with the grave public health threat posed by cigarettes—if only Congress would do its part. Fine. Let's get on with it. Agreement is fairly widespread, including among some in the tobacco industry itself, on the fundamental elements that should go into FDA regulation of tobacco products.

## Nicotine Is a Drug

We can't hide from the fact that nicotine in cigarettes is a drug. The nation's most important consumer protection agency that regulates all other legal addictive drugs should regulate this drug. It is the right fit. We've been through the hardest part already. Two years ago [1998], when tobacco legislation was before Congress, the only section of that bill[1] not challenged during the debate was the FDA portion. Senators of both parties, by and large, were satisfied that the FDA part was right.

What are the basic elements of FDA regulation on which most of us can agree without any further delay? First, tobacco can be regulated as a drug, but under a flexible standard as a unique product, in either the existing or separate section of the FDA statutes. That should allay the Supreme Court's basic fear—that the FDA would ban cigarettes if they were regulated under existing drug and medical device statutes.

Second, we must have constraints on marketing aimed at young people. Most adult smokers start when they're underage. We need to codify the FDA regulations that were aimed at reducing access and the appeal of cigarettes to young people.

1. The National Tobacco Policy and Youth Smoking Reduction Act included increasing cigarette taxes by $1.10 over five years, capping the amount of damages the tobacco industry would pay plaintiffs at $6.5 billion a year, limit the cigarette industry's ability to advertise, imposing up to $3.5 billion a year in fines if youth smoking does not meet agreed-on goals, and providing $28.5 billion in relief for tobacco farmers, in addition to giving the Food and Drug Administration (FDA) power to regulate nicotine.

Third, we need to give the agency the ability to remove harmful ingredients, to monitor the manufacturing process and to modify the product based on the best science.

Fourth, we need adequate funding and guidelines for smoking-cessation research.

And, finally, we need to put a regulatory process in place that encourages companies to speed up efforts to develop, manufacture and market "safer" cigarettes, if that is possible.

## FDA Should Help Cure Diseases

This will be a difficult task. A member of the House leadership said recently that the FDA should help cure diseases. He's right. No bigger cure exists than to prevent future generations from dying from this scourge.

Americans believe the tobacco industry wields undue influence in Congress. I believe, however, if it came to a vote today, most members of Congress would want to do something meaningful about tobacco. Recently, I debated a Philip Morris executive over the possible outlines of FDA regulation of cigarettes. We largely agreed on the fundamentals I just described. If the two of us can agree, surely Congress can do something in an honest and straightforward way that the public will understand.

---

### FDA Oversight Is Necessary

The FDA [Food and Drug Administration] is the only government agency that can provide comprehensive oversight of all aspects of tobacco-product development and marketing, including the companies' use of dangerous chemical additives, their nicotine manipulation and their advertising and promotional efforts that attract kids. Compared to Congress or the state legislatures, the FDA also has the ability to modify its regulations swiftly to counteract changes in tobacco-industry tactics and more effectively protect children from the hazards of tobacco use, and is less likely to be corrupted or impeded by tobacco-company money and influence.

Bill Novelli, *Insight on the News*, May 10, 1999.

---

The effort thus far by the FDA has accomplished a lot. The agency's courage emboldened others to enter the tobacco wars in the past five years. The public now knows with certainty that nicotine is addictive, that the industry manipulates and controls nicotine levels and that the industry targeted young smokers to replace adult smokers who die prematurely.

There is a growing sense in this country that the tobacco industry has lied to and manipulated the public for years. In the coming years, millions of young people, knowing of the industry's crass deception, will make the decision not to start smoking. Thousands of adults will sit on juries and punish the industry for decades of lies and manipulation. It really won't take much to get started on FDA regulation. We've already been through the hardest part of the debate. Now it's time to act.

*"If given regulatory authority over cigarettes, the FDA would . . . risk . . . accurately being labeled our 'national nanny' . . . simply because it seems very unlikely that the FDA would stop with measures aimed at children."*

# The Food and Drug Administration Should Not Regulate Tobacco Products

Michael DeBow

Michael DeBow contends in the following viewpoint that Congress should not grant the Food and Drug Administration (FDA) the authority to regulate tobacco products because to do so would give the federal government power not granted to it by the Constitution and further expand the nanny state. DeBow insists that regulation of tobacco is a function that states perform more effectively than the federal government. Further, if the FDA is allowed to regulate tobacco, it will not stop with measures aimed at reducing children's access to tobacco products but will ultimately seek to control tobacco use by adults as well. Michael DeBow is a professor of law at Samford University in Birmingham, Alabama.

As you read, consider the following questions:

1. When did the FDA announce its intention to begin regulating cigarettes, according to the author?
2. In the author's opinion, what would every substantial restrictive move against adult smoking do?

S hould the Food and Drug Administration, or FDA, have regulatory authority over cigarettes? Certainly the burden of persuasion should be on the proponents of this expansion of the FDA's powers. I do not think that they can bear this burden for the reasons explored below—one narrowly constitutional, the other broadly constitutional. This controversy dates back to August 1995 when for the first time in its 90-odd-year history, the FDA announced its intention to begin regulating cigarettes. Roughly one year later, the agency published a "final" set of regulations for cigarettes which, with supporting materials, ran to more than 900 pages in the *Federal Register*. The FDA framed the regulations entirely in terms of "restricting the sale and distribution of cigarettes and smokeless tobacco to protect children and adolescents." The primary provisions of the regulations include a mandatory age of 18 for cigarette purchases, a ban on cigarette vending machines and self-service displays in almost all circumstances, a prohibition on the distribution of free samples and a number of limitations on the advertising of cigarettes.

The cigarette companies challenged the regulations in court, arguing that the agency had overstepped its statutory authority. Last summer [1998], the U.S. Court of Appeals for the 4th Circuit agreed with the companies' argument that the federal Food, Drug and Cosmetic Act, or FDCA, does not grant the FDA authority to regulate cigarettes as "drugs" or "devices." In January [1999], the Department of Justice petitioned the Supreme Court to review the 4th Circuit's ruling, with an eye toward overruling it and thus establishing FDA authority to regulate cigarettes.

The Supreme Court likely will decide whether to review the 4th Circuit's decision in the next couple of months.[1] If the court decides not to review the ruling—or if it decides to uphold the 4th Circuit—then Congress may consider amending the FDCA to empower the FDA to regulate cigarettes. Already the White House is on record as favoring "comprehensive tobacco legislation to confirm the FDA's authority and take this matter out of the courtroom."

1. The U.S. Supreme Court decided in March 2000 that the Food and Drug Administration (FDA) lacked jurisdiction over tobacco products because Congress had never authorized the FDA to regulate tobacco as a drug or medical device.

## Congress Should Ban FDA Regulation

But there are two good reasons why Congress shouldn't act to grant jurisdiction over cigarettes to the FDA. The first has to do with federalism, and the second with the need to guard against further expansions of the nanny state—which already has expanded greatly in the recent crusade against cigarette use. While neither reason alone provides a definitive answer to FDA's designs on cigarette regulation, considered together they constitute a strong argument against such an expansion of the agency's authority.

Under our Constitution, the government of the United States is vertically divided between a federal government of express powers and 50 state governments with the residual powers of government. Ideally, the federal government would move into an area of regulation only when: 1) there is a demonstrated public need for regulation, 2) there is a constitutional basis for federal involvement in the particular issue and 3) the states' attempts to regulate have been ineffective. Normally these three requirements are satisfied only when commercial activities within one state have a negative effect on residents of other states. Put another way, the more "local" a problem, the more appropriate it is to address it through state or local government action, as opposed to federal-government action.

## State Regulation Is Best

States long have been active in the regulation of cigarette sales. In particular, every state already has a statute that defines the legal age for buying cigarettes and prescribes penalties for sales to underage buyers. The FDA recognized this fact, but pointed to what it saw as an unacceptably high level of illegal sales to minors as justifying federal intervention.

Let us agree that fewer sales to minors would be in the public interest. Which level of government—state or federal—is better positioned to make a judgment about how to police the age requirement? This seems an overwhelmingly local problem in which a federal presence is unnecessary. Moreover, it seems unrealistic, to say the least, to imagine that the federal law-enforcement system will devote substantial resources to tracking down and punishing careless or amoral convenience-store clerks and the like. The realities of federal law enforcement—particularly the problem of scarce resources and more serious criminals to catch—suggest that the call for the FDA to get into policing cigarette sales to minors is more grandstanding than a serious proposal.

Further, federal preemption of the states might well be counterproductive: By subjecting the entire country to a uniform federal approach to the problem of underage sales, FDA regulation would deprive us of the so-called laboratory of the states that exists whenever states are left to their own devices in regulatory matters. With 50 states pursuing different enforcement strategies aimed at underage sales, we might learn more quickly what works and what doesn't. A single federal enforcement regime would not yield this knowledge.

## Smoking Is a Local Problem

Further, many of the other industry practices the FDA seeks to regulate also are quite local in nature—the use of vending machines and self-service displays, for example. Although there are a few geographic areas in which minors might cross state lines to avail themselves of a more permissive regulatory environment, this is quite a weak basis for federal intervention.

In short, the local nature of the problem of sales to underage smokers argues strongly in favor of leaving that problem to the states. On a related point, the FDA regulations would restrict certain advertising practices that it argues appeal to children and adolescents. Even assuming that such regulatory measures eventually would depress youth demand for cigarettes, this aspect of the proposed FDA regulatory scheme has been rendered largely moot by the November 1998 settlement of the states' lawsuits against the tobacco companies. The states' settlement includes a number of restrictions on advertising—including limitations on billboards and on the distribution of free samples and other merchandise bearing tobacco logos. The FDA's attempt to regulate cigarette advertising no longer is necessary or even advisable, if it ever was.

If no federal action is necessary or desirable with respect to either cigarette sales to underage smokers or cigarette advertising aimed at young people, what possible justification is left for the FDA to enter into the regulation of the cigarette industry?

## Prohibitionist Thinking

It is difficult to look at the nation's preoccupation with smoking and public policies relating to smoking during the last few years and not conclude that there is a strong element of prohibitionist thinking in the antismoking camp. The likely future trajectory of the FDA's entry into cigarette regulation should be considered in light of this fact. If given regulatory authority over cigarettes, the FDA would run the risk of accurately being labeled our "national nanny" . . . simply because it seems very unlikely that the FDA would stop with measures aimed at children. Instead, the FDA would face further pressure from the antismoking lobby to limit adult access to cigarette advertising and to cigarettes. Proposals to make cigarettes a prescription-only drug already have been floated. Certainly we've not seen the last of the antitobacco crusade or calls for government "action" to limit adult smoking.

---

### Food and Drug Administration Regulation Will Not Reduce Smoking

Giving a federal bureaucracy undefined control over tobacco companies will not reduce cigarette smoking in the U.S. Rather, to achieve this public health goal, we must hold the tobacco industry accountable for its behavior of marketing an inherently dangerous product without complete disclosure.

Elizabeth M. Whelan, American Council on Science and Health, March 22, 2000. www.acsh.org.

---

It is common for bureaucrats to seek more turf, more employees, larger budgets, more clout. This bureaucratic imperative, combined with pressure from the antismoking lobby, is likely to push a future FDA to impose more and more restrictions on cigarettes as time goes by. As a result, the FDA will increase the cost of smoking and otherwise infringe on the ability of adults to smoke.

If this happens, the nation will be flirting with a form of

prohibition quite similar to the alcohol prohibition of the 1920s and 1930s. A very widely used product that is inexpensive and easily concealed is difficult to legislate against effectively. Every substantial restrictive move against adult smoking would increase the incentives people have to buy and sell tobacco products on illegal black markets. If the FDA preempts the states in the area of cigarettes, we will run the risk of moving toward a national policy of prohibition, with all that entails. And the fact that the states could not alter such a policy would deprive us of federalism's laboratory of the states here, too. We would not know if, as a result of stringent anti-smoking policies, we were close to the outbreak of widespread black-market activity or not. Conversely, in a state-based regulatory regime, some states would be stricter than others and would generate information about how far a state can push its regulatory agenda without prompting large increases in black-market activity.

## The Threat of a National Nanny

But the potential for FDA regulations directed at adult smokers raises a still broader issue: Do we want our federal (or state) government to take aggressive steps to convince us—even coerce us—to abandon unhealthy habits? In answering this question, keep in mind that smoking is not the only unhealthy habit in modern American life. (My own diet and exercise shortcomings are painfully obvious to me.) What should the government do here? Are we ready for a national nanny?

Writing in the 1830s, Alexis de Tocqueville speculated about the "sort of despotism democratic nations have to fear." He worried that democratic politics would result in "an immense and tutelary power" which would stand above the citizens and "take upon itself alone to secure their gratifications and to watch over their fate. That power is absolute, minute, regular, provident, and mild." This government would cover "the surface of society with a network of small complicated rules, minute and uniform." The result would be a "power [that] does not destroy" but rather "compresses, enervates, extinguishes, and stupefies a people, till each nation is reduced to nothing better than a flock of timid and industrious animals, of which the government is the shepherd." A decision to deny the FDA regulatory power over cigarettes would leave the states perfectly free to make their own efforts to discourage teen smoking and seems to me a very advisable tactic in avoiding Tocqueville's worst-case scenario.

"*Of all intervention measures related to demand, price has been shown to be the single most effective means of changing tobacco use behavior.*"

# Increasing Cigarette Taxes Will Help Reduce Tobacco Use

Michelle Leverett, Marice Ashe, Susan Gerard, Jim Jenson, and Trevor Woollery

Increasing cigarette taxes encourages current smokers to quit and reduces the number of people—particularly teens— who start the habit, the authors maintain in the following viewpoint. They argue that a 10 percent price increase reduces cigarette consumption by children and teens by as much as 8 percent. Michelle Leverett is director and health officer for the Baltimore County Health Department; Marice Ashe is director of the Public Health Institute of Oakland, California; Susan Gerard is a member of the Arizona senate; Jim Jenson is a member of the Nebraska legislature; and Trevor Woollery is an economist at the Centers for Disease Control and Prevention.

As you read, consider the following questions:
1. According to the authors, what measures—in addition to tax increases—have been found to be effective in reducing the demand for tobacco?
2. What objections to cigarette tax increases do opponents typically raise, in the authors' opinion?
3. In what two ways does cigarette smuggling occur, according to the authors?

Michelle Leverett et al., "Tobacco Use: The Impact of Prices," *Journal of Law, Medicine and Ethics*, Fall 2002. Copyright © 2002 by American Society of Law, Medicine and Ethics. Reproduced by permission.

Estimates show that smoking caused over $150 billion in annual health-related economic losses from 1995 to 1999, a figure that includes an average annual productivity loss of $81.9 billion and medical expenditures in excess of $75.5 billion in 1998. Given the health and economic burden of tobacco, interventions are necessary to curb the epidemic of smoking and tobacco use. The measures that reduce the demand for tobacco products have proven most effective in reducing smoking prevalence, limiting youth initiation, and increasing cessation rates. Some successful measures include increasing prices by such means as imposing higher cigarette taxes and non-price measures such as providing consumer information, banning cigarette advertising and promotion, and mandating warning labels and restrictions on public smoking. Greater public access to nicotine replacement products and other cessation therapies have been shown to have an impact on the demand for cigarettes.

Of all intervention measures related to demand, price has been shown to be the single most effective means of changing tobacco use behavior. A 1985 Philip Morris International internal document states that

> It is clear that in the US, and in most countries in which we operate, tax is becoming a major threat to our existence. Of all the concerns, there is on—taxation—that alarms us the most. While marketing restrictions and public and passive smoking (restrictions) do depress volume, in our experience taxation depresses it much more severely. Our concern for taxation is, therefore, central to our thinking about smoking and health. It has historically been the area to which we have devoted most resources and for the foreseeable future, I think things will stay that way almost everywhere.

Higher cigarette taxes promote cessation among current adult smokers and reduce cigarette consumption by adult smokers who continue the habit, helping these smokers move towards cessation. Estimates imply that a ten percent price increase reduces overall cigarette consumption in this group by four percent, with approximately half of the impact resulting from reductions in the number of smokers.

Young adults are about twice as price-sensitive as adults. Estimates show that a ten percent price increase reduces overall young adult consumption by eight percent, with approximately half of the impact resulting from reductions in the number of young adult smokers; the probability of daily smoking initiation among young adults would decline by about 10 percent.

Children and adolescents are about three times more sensitive to cigarette price changes than are adults, with estimates indicating that a ten percent price increase eliminates the smoking habit of this group by six to seven percent. Higher taxes are particularly effective in preventing young experimenters from progressing to regular smoking, addiction, and, for many, a premature death caused by tobacco use. Because children are highly price-sensitive and 90 percent of all smokers start as teens, higher taxes can sharply reduce smoking in the long run.

Higher tobacco taxes also generate substantial revenues that can be used to support comprehensive state tobacco control programs. Revenues from tobacco tax increases fired many of the longest running and most effective state tobacco use reduction programs, including those in California and Massachusetts. Such programs lead to significant declines in the public health toll caused by tobacco. For every dollar spent on tobacco control, over three dollars are saved in avoided direct medical costs.

## Objections Are Overcome by Facts

Opponents of tobacco tax increases typically raise four objections. These objections focus on the potential negative effects of an increase on current levels of tobacco tax revenues, the cost to tobacco users in particular, the possible job losses associated with reduced tobacco consumption, and the fact that tobacco products available via the Internet escape the same tax burden. The facts argue against these objections. To date, no decrease in overall cigarette tax revenues has resulted from an imposition of higher cigarette taxes in any state; to the contrary, overall tobacco tax revenues have always increased. While it is possible that job losses may be associated with higher cigarette taxes, these losses are minimal and temporary in nature. Moreover, money not spent on tobacco products due to higher costs is diverted to other parts of the economy, thus creating jobs to offset any tobacco-related job losses. In addition, poor people, the population most adversely impacted by the health consequences of tobacco use, are much more responsive than higher income persons to increases in tobacco taxes—thus they are beneficiaries rather than victims of increased tobacco taxes. In the United States, estimates indicate that smoking in households below median income level is about 70 percent more responsive to price than households above median income level.

---

## Higher Taxes Mean Fewer Smokers

This month [July 2002] Pennsylvania increased its cigarette tax from 31 cents to $1 a pack and New Jersey's went from 80 cents to $1.50, causing many smokers to rethink their lifestyles.

They are part of a nationwide trend: Four states raised cigarette taxes in 2001, and 16 states, New York City, and Puerto Rico increased their taxes this year [2002]. . . .

"In several states, consumption declined 20 percent or more, and new revenues in the millions of dollars were still realized," the [Smokeless States National Tobacco Policy Initiative] reported in a study presented . . . at the annual meeting of the National Conference of State Legislatures in Denver.

Aparna Surendran, *Philadelphia Inquirer,* July 30, 2002.

---

The issue of the availability of tobacco products via the Internet is more problematic. Internet sales represent a new and growing challenge for tobacco control and for policy makers. The gains made by limiting access to tobacco products through imposition of higher prices via increasing the federal tax and the various state taxes; efforts to increase access to information about the health effects of tobacco through warning labels; the imposition of advertising and promotion bans; and laws limiting youth access to tobacco products—all can be seriously compromised and undermined if the use of the Internet effectively lowers tobacco prices and increases youth access to tobacco products. The evidence based on this new source of access is limited but growing. However, the available evidence indicates that Internet sales could be a threat if proper policy measures are not put in place to protect the nation's youth by limiting their access. . . .

## More Faulty Claims

Despite tobacco industry claims to the contrary, smuggling is not invariably linked to higher taxes on tobacco. Data on the price of cigarettes and smuggling rates destroy the connection between taxes and increased crime. For example, countries with low cigarette prices (Spain at $1.20 per pack and Italy at $2.07 per pack) have high smuggling rates. And countries with high cigarette prices (Sweden at $4.97 per pack and Norway at $6.27 per pack) have low smuggling rates.

In the United States, despite a relatively well paid and organized law enforcement system, some smuggling occurs, either through organized crime or through the interstate purchase of tobacco products by individuals. While losses to smuggling directed by organized crime are difficult to estimate, it is estimated that approximately $400 million of state tax revenue is lost annually on a national basis due to the interstate purchase of cigarettes by individuals. Research shows that such purchases are mainly confined to communities bordering a state with lower tobacco prices. . . .

## Criticisms Notwithstanding, Taxes Work

Increases in excise taxes are an effective tool in the public health community's efforts to reduce smoking, particularly among youth. The adoption of excise tax increases on tobacco products requires persistence, both in enacting the increase and in ensuring that the revenues are used to protect the public's health. Contrary to the arguments of opponents of such tax increases, the smuggling of tobacco products and the sale of tobacco over the Internet have not yet diminished the efficacy of excise tax increases.

*"Higher cigarette taxes will simply impose extremely regressive burdens on the poorest members of society who can least afford to bear the cost."*

# Increasing Cigarette Taxes on Tobacco Will Not Reduce Tobacco Use

W. Kip Viscusi

Increasing tobacco taxes is not an effective method of reducing cigarette consumption, particularly among children and teens, W. Kip Viscusi contends in the following viewpoint. Increased cigarette taxes have the greatest impact on the very poor, he argues, not on children, teens, or the majority of adult smokers. He insists that efforts to reduce smoking should instead work to establish nonsmoking areas and smoking lounges in public places so that nonsmokers are not harmed. W. Kip Viscusi is a professor of law and economics at Harvard Law School.

As you read, consider the following questions:
1. What does Viscusi argue is the basis for prohibitionist concerns about smoking?
2. What is the public's perception of the harmfulness of secondhand smoke, in the author's opinion?
3. According to Viscusi, why will smoking rates continue to decline, even in the absence of any additional policy interventions?

W. Kip Viscusi, "The New Cigarette Paternalism," *Regulation*, Winter 2003.

S moking is by far the largest single risk that most people take. Perhaps in part because of that prominence, smoking has been the target of a wide variety of regulations and legal actions. The controversy over tobacco products is at least four centuries old, but it has been largely over the past half-century that the diverse wave of public policy initiatives against tobacco products has emerged.

Within a standard economic framework of consumer choice, there would seem to be little impetus for broadly based government efforts to discourage smoking. The risks of smoking are largely borne by the consumers who choose those products. To the extent that smoking harms others, the externalities can often be addressed through focused policy measures such as non-smoking areas.

Over the past decade, cigarettes have been under increasing assault on two fronts. First, there have been claims that the underlying rationality of smoking decisions is in doubt and that smokers need to be protected from themselves. Second, policy concerns over exposures to tobacco smoke escalated as government agencies suggested that smoking does in fact impose considerable health harms on others.

Many anti-smoking advocates would like to prohibit smoking altogether. The prohibitionist concerns may stem from religious fervor, as some have long viewed smoking and drinking as evil. Other prohibitionist concerns stem from a sense of paternalism. The demographic distribution of smoking is more concentrated among the less well educated, such as those in blue-collar occupations rather than the white-collar professionals who tend to shape public policy. Given that policymakers themselves tend not to smoke, they often view any decision to smoke as mistaken. In their view, some form of irrationality must account for the fact that smokers' choices are different from what the policymakers would choose to do.

## Smoking Risks Are Known

It was not until the 1964 report by the U.S. Department of Health, Education, and Welfare that the U.S. government announced a consensus that smoking does significantly increase the risk of lung cancer. Press coverage of the report was tremendous, and the U.S. Congress required that, beginning in 1966, cigarette packs had to bear on-product warnings. The mandatory warning for a consumer product was truly a watershed event; before that time, warnings were primarily restricted to products that posed imminent dangers that typically were fatal. The widespread warnings that we now take for granted simply did not exist. Rather, cigarettes were singled out as a high-risk commodity that was dangerous even if used in the manner intended by the manufacturer.

Policy efforts to inform smokers of the hazards of smoking did not end with the 1966 warnings. There have been two revisions of the cigarette warnings, and the Surgeon General and other public health officials have continued to publicize the risks of smoking over the past four decades. . . .

Public knowledge of the risks of smoking is consequently not a recent development. Research on other forms of risk indicates that people tend to overestimate highly publicized risks. Given the tremendous publicity that smoking risks have received, one would expect that people would tend to overestimate the risks of smoking rather than underestimate the dangers. . . .

## Secondhand Smoke

For years, people regarded environmental tobacco smoke as a smelly annoyance. Beginning in the 1990s, government agencies began to suggest that the scientific evidence indicated that environmental tobacco smoke could also cause cancer and heart disease. The character of the stakes involved in smoking had changed considerably, as had the moral authority of non-smokers. The result was a widespread belief that smokers were harming not only themselves but nonsmokers as well.

The watershed event in the assault against secondhand smoke was EPA's (Environmental Protection Agency) designation of environmental tobacco smoke as a group-A carcinogen. No longer was the concern pertaining to environmental tobacco smoke based on aesthetics; lives were at risk as well. Careful review of the studies of the lung cancer-environmental tobacco smoke linkage indicates that none of the studies has ever demonstrated a relationship that passes the usual tests of statistical significance. As a result, there have been a number of critiques of the EPA analysis. . . .

The federal judiciary has rejected the EPA study of passive smoking as well, notably in the 1998 decision for *Flue-Cured Tobacco Cooperative Stabilization Corp. et al. v. U.S. Environmental Protection Agency.* The court threw out the EPA study for several reasons: "EPA's study selection is disturbing. First, there is evidence in the record supporting the accusation that the EPA 'cherry-picked' its data." Moreover, the court found that "using its normal methodology and its selected studies, EPA did not demonstrate a statistically significant association between [environmental tobacco smoke] and lung cancer." Moreover, "EPA could not produce statistically significant results with its selected studies."

## Exaggerated Perception

Nevertheless, the public's perception regarding the dangers of passive smoking is far in excess of the risks that actually may be present. In a study of the environmental tobacco risk perceptions that I undertook in Spain, the Spanish population believes that 25 out of 100 members of the population would get lung cancer because of exposures to environmental tobacco smoke, and a similar number would get heart disease because of passive smoking exposures. The dangers of environmental tobacco smoke are consequently believed to be tantamount to the risks posed by the Black Plague.

Research studies continue to explore the possibility of the linkage of passive smoking exposures to lung cancer, heart disease, and other ailments. However, even if such linkages can be established, they do not imply that there should be a higher tax on cigarettes. The solution is to adopt smoking restrictions that prevent nonsmokers from being exposed to environmental tobacco smoke. Ideally, such policies should also attempt to accommodate the interests of smokers by providing for smoking lounges.

Smoking restrictions have become increasingly prevalent throughout the United States. Large businesses are particularly likely to have adopted formal smoking restriction policies. Many states have done so as well. By 1998, 31 states had adopted restrictions on smoking in restaurants, and 23 states imposed statewide restrictions on smoking in indoor arenas. The emergence of targeted policies to address environmental tobacco smoke represents a more sensible solution to those hazards than penalizing smoking activity more broadly. Concerns about environmental tobacco smoke consequently should not serve as a rationale for taxing cigarettes more generally.

## Cigarette Tax Policy

The tax component of cigarettes is substantial. As of 2001, the federal tax rate on cigarettes was 34¢ per pack, and the average state tax was 40.8¢ per pack. The state of New York imposed a high value of $1.11 per pack, which has since been topped by additional taxes imposed by the city of New York. An additional 40¢ per pack of the cigarette price is attributable to the penalties levied as a result of the Master Settlement Agreement[1] as well as the settlement with four additional states that were not parties to that agreement. The result is that the average national retail price of cigarettes is $3.57 per pack for full-price cigarettes and $3.37 per pack if one includes generic cigarettes in the averaging.

Cigarette taxes fall predominantly on the very poor. The usual concerns about regressive taxes involve those that are regressive in percentage terms, that is, the poor pay a higher percentage of their income in taxes than do the wealthy. Cigarette taxes are actually so regressive that the poor pay a much higher absolute level of taxes than do the wealthy. In 1990, people who made under $10,000 per year paid almost twice as much in cigarette taxes as those who made $50,000 and above. The people who will bear the cigarette taxes are not the legislators who enact them but rather the janitors and support staff for the legislature. The stark regressivity of cigarette taxes has often led to some hesitancy in imposing cigarette taxes at even higher levels. . . .

When the discussions were ongoing with respect to the settlement of the litigation by the states against the tobacco

1. Cigarette companies reached a settlement with forty-six states over claims that the tobacco industry had lied about the adverse health effects of smoking. In November 1998, the tobacco companies agreed to pay participating states a total of $206 billion over the next twenty-five years.

industry, the attorneys general invoked many fervent pleas that they needed the money to protect youths against the dangers of smoking. Surely, that is a policy objective on which everyone can agree. However, the actual allocation of the windfall received by the states has done little to combat youth smoking. Almost every other possible use for the funds has taken priority. Some states spent the money to reduce crowding in public schools, others spent it on rebuilding roads and bridges or on sidewalk repair. In perhaps the most appalling use of the funds, the mayor of Los Angeles proposed using the windfall to pay for the legal defenses of police officers accused of allegedly planting drugs and weapons on subjects and either beating or shooting unarmed suspects.

Beattie. © 1998 by Daytona Beach News Journal. Reproduced by permission of Copley News Service.

In much the same vein, Gruber has suggested that boosting cigarette taxes is needed to deter youth smoking. A frequent argument for using taxes to deter underage smoking is the belief that youths exhibit a higher price elasticity for cigarettes—an empirical claim that is a matter of some dispute among economists. Many researchers have failed to find a difference in the price elasticity of youths.

The more fundamental problem is that the policy proposal

118

is too blunt to address the youth smoking problem sensibly. One of the results of the tobacco settlement has been the enactment of laws throughout the United States prohibiting those under the age of 18 from buying cigarettes. Purchasing cigarettes is now illegal for youths, which makes proposals to crank up the tax to deter youth smoking misdirected.

## Few Youths Buy Cigarettes for Themselves

Underage smokers continue to exist notwithstanding the regulations. It is often hypothesized that the weak link is retailers, such as those who operate convenience stores. If that is the case, then presumably a higher tax on cigarettes would affect purchases of cigarettes by youths. A 1998 California survey that took place around the period when many of the age requirements took effect indicated that very few youths actually purchased cigarettes themselves. Only eight percent of eighth graders who smoke cigarettes bought them themselves, and only 10 percent of 10th graders indicated that they bought them themselves. Underage smokers instead get their cigarettes from friends, family members, older friends who purchase cigarettes for them, and by stealing cigarettes. Most of those sources of cigarettes will not be particularly responsive to higher cigarette prices.

Imposing higher taxes on cigarettes for all smokers also imposes costs that will fall largely on adult smokers rather than youths. Empirical estimates peg the percentage of cigarettes smoked by underage smokers as being roughly three percent of all cigarettes sold. Using the youth smoking hook to justify broadly based taxes consequently will impose costs largely on people who have nothing whatsoever to do with youth smoking. Targeted interventions, including enforcement of age restrictions on cigarette purchases and other youth smoking policies, are more appropriate forms of intervention. . . .

## Targeted Efforts Work Best

The impetus for boosting cigarette taxes is likely to continue because most voters will not bear the cost. Those who will pay are the minority of the population who are smokers. Smokers are disadvantaged additionally by the fact that they tend to vote with a lower frequency than do nonsmokers. Higher cigarette taxes will simply impose extremely regressive burdens on the poorest members of society who can least afford to bear the cost.

Policymakers should focus on more targeted efforts to address smoking matters of concern. Age restrictions on smoking, the establishment of non-smoking areas and smoking lounges, and similar measures represent the kinds of interventions that are structured in a way that will generate the desired benefits without imposing costs on entire populations of smokers.

Even in the absence of any additional policy interventions, smoking rates will continue to decline just as they have over the past half-century. As individual wealth rises, the value associated with health risks increases as well. People consequently will be less willing to bear risks as they become more affluent. Market forces alone will continue to generate a decline in smoking, but they will do so in a way that is respectful to individual preferences and the choices that people make.

"*All of the commercially available forms of nicotine replacement therapy are effective. . . . They increase quit rates approximately 1.5 to 2 fold regardless of setting.*"

# Nicotine Replacement Therapy May Help Some Smokers Quit

Lisa J. Diefenbach and Patrick O. Smith

Nicotine replacement therapy (NRT) can increase quit rates by 150 to 200 percent, Lisa J. Diefenbach and Patrick O. Smith claim in the following viewpoint. According to the authors, all forms of NRT (gum, transdermal patch, spray, inhaler, and lozenge) are equally effective, so the choice of which form to use should be made based on the smoker's preference and level of nicotine dependence. Lisa J. Diefenbach and Patrick O. Smith are members of the department of family medicine at the University of Mississippi Medical Center.

As you read, consider the following questions:
1. According to the authors, what is the effect of nicotine gum on weight gain?
2. In the authors' opinion, which smokers should be preferentially directed to use NRT?
3. If a single form of NRT is not effective, what do the authors contend smokers should do?

Lisa J. Diefenbach and Patrick O. Smith, "What Is the Most Effective Nicotine Replacement Therapy?" *Journal of Family Practice*, vol. 52, June 2003, pp. 492–94. Copyright © 2003 by *Journal of Family Practice*. Reproduced by permission.

No single nicotine replacement therapy is most effective for all smokers. All forms of nicotine replacement therapy (gum, transdermal patch, spray, inhaler, and lozenge) are equally effective, increasing smoking cessation rates by about 150% to 200%.

A *Cochrane Review* found that 17% of smokers who had used nicotine replacement therapy successfully quit at follow-up vs 10% of smokers in the control group. Except in special circumstances (medical contraindications, smoking <10 cigarettes daily, pregnancy, or breastfeeding), all smokers attempting to quit should be offered nicotine replacement therapy.

Higher doses of nicotine gum or lozenge (4 mg vs 2 mg) increase quit rates in heavy smokers. Use of high-dose patches (>21 mg) may benefit heavy smokers or those relapsing due to nicotine withdrawal. For relapsed smokers, combination therapy improves long-term abstinence rates (estimated abstinence 28.6% vs 17.4% for monotherapy).

## Combination Therapy Is More Effective

A *Cochrane Review* of 110 trials evaluating the efficacy of nicotine replacement therapy in 35,600 smokers found higher quit rates among heavy smokers using 4-mg compared with 2-mg nicotine gum. However, patients often chew too few pieces of nicotine gum daily, resulting in underdosing. Smokers should use the gum on a fixed schedule (at least 1 piece every 1 to 2 hours). The *Cochrane Review* finds borderline evidence of a small benefit in abstinence rates with higher-dose nicotine patches (>21 mg/24 hr or 15 mg/16 hr) for heavy or relapsed smokers. Combining methods that maintain constant drug levels (transdermal patch) with those having more rapid effects (gum, spray, inhaler, lozenge) is more effective than monotherapy. Reserve combination therapy for smokers who relapse following monotherapy.

Regarding concerns about weight gain, all nicotine replacement therapies delay but do not prevent weight gain. There is a dose-response relationship between nicotine gum and weight gain: smokers who use more gum gain less weight.

Although abstinence rates are comparable across the 5 available forms of nicotine replacement, smokers unwilling to give up oral and behavioral rituals of smoking may perceive the inhaler as being more helpful.

Decisions about the best form of therapy can be based on patient preference, on degree of nicotine dependence (a Fagerstrom Test of Nicotine Dependence Scale score [greater than or equal to] 5 [Table 1], or habitually smoking the first cigarette within 30 minutes of awakening), or nicotine replacement therapy history, which includes number and outcome of previous quit attempts, specific method used, duration, side effects, and proper usage.

## NRT Almost Doubles Quit Rates

The *Cochrane Review* states: "All of the commercially available forms of nicotine replacement therapy are effective as part of a strategy to promote smoking cessation. They increase quit rates approximately 1.5 to 2 fold regardless of setting. Use of nicotine replacement therapy should be preferentially directed to smokers who are motivated to quit,

## Table 1. Fagerström Test for Level of Nicotine Dependence (Abridged)

**How soon after waking do you smoke first cigarette?** ___ **Points**

Less than 5 minutes: 3 points

5 to 30 minutes: 2 points

31 to 60 minutes: 1 point

**How many cigarettes do you smoke per day?** ___ **Points**

More than 30 per day: 3 points

21 to 30 per day: 2 points

11 to 20 per day: 1 point

___ **Total Points**

**Interpretation**

| Total points | Level of dependence | Nicotine replacement therapy |
|---|---|---|
| 5–6 points | heavy nicotine dependence | consider 21-mg nicotine patch |
| 3–4 points | moderate nicotine dependence | consider 14-mg nicotine patch |
| 0–2 points | light nicotine dependence | consider 7-mg nicotine patch or no patch |

and have high levels of nicotine dependency. Choice of which form to use should reflect patient needs, tolerability and cost considerations. Patches are likely to be easier to use than gum or nasal spray in primary care settings."

The US Department of Health and Human Services Clinical Practice Guideline states: "All patients attempting to quit should be encouraged to use effective pharmacotherapies for smoking cessation except in the presence of special circumstances." Heavy smokers should use 4-mg nicotine gum. Combining the nicotine patch with a self-administered form of nicotine replacement therapy (gum or nicotine nasal spray) is more efficacious than a single form of therapy. Patients should be encouraged to use combined treatments if unable to quit using a single form of first-line pharmacotherapy.

Now that nicotine replacement therapy is available over the counter, prescribers may not consider or discuss delivery options with patients as much as they did in the past. As this Clinical Inquiry illustrates, there are situations when one approach may be recommended over another.

For example, the relapsed smoker who has tried 1 nicotine replacement product may not even be aware that other methods, including combination therapy, are possible. Considering the enormous potential health improvement that is achieved through smoking cessation, this may be one of the most important topics to revisit regularly with patients.

*"Although pharmaceutical aids . . . helped
moderate-to-heavy smokers discontinue
using cigarettes longer, they were not
associated with a clinically meaningful long-
term improvement in successful cessation and
no benefit was observed in light smokers."*

# Nicotine Replacement Therapy Is Ineffective

*Formulary*

In the following viewpoint editors from *Formulary* argue
that nicotine replacement therapy (NRT) is ineffective as a
long-term smoking cessation aid. Based on results from
three surveys of smokers in California, the editors conclude
that while moderate-to-heavy smokers may refrain from
smoking for a few days longer using NRT, no improvement
in long-term cessation was found. Further, light smokers
were not helped at all by NRT. *Formulary* is a monthly clinical journal for members of pharmacy and therapeutic com-
mittees at hospitals, managed care settings, and within the
Veterans Administration system.

As you read, consider the following questions:
1. In the authors' opinion, how did insurance coverage
   affect NRT use?
2. According to the 1999 survey, what percentage of NRT
   users also used some type of behavior modification
   assistance, according to the authors?
3. To what do the authors attribute at least part of the high
   relapse rate of smokers using NRT?

Formulary, "Nicotine Replacement Therapy Is Ineffective as a Long-Term
Smoking Cessation Aid," *Formulary*, vol. 37, October 2002, p. 501. Copyright
© 2002 by Advanstar Communications, Inc. Reproduced by permission.

Nicotine replacement therapy (NRT)—ie, nicotine gum, patch, or inhalant—appears to be an ineffective long-term smoking cessation aid, according to results of a new study. Researchers conducted three surveys of tobacco smokers in California. Surveys were conducted in 1992, 1996, and 1999 and included 5,247, 9,725, and 6,412 respondents, respectively. Response rates ranged from 68% to 73% across the three surveys. The surveys investigated the rates of cessation attempts ([greater than or equal to] 1 day) among smokers, the use of pharmaceutical cessation aids, and cessation success.

Across all three surveys, smoking cessation attempts lasting a day or longer improved during each survey period—from 38% in the 1992 survey, to 56% in 1996, to 61.5% in 1999. Similarly, the use of NRT increased from 9.3% in 1992 to 14% in 1999 (p < 0.001). In 1999, 17.2% of respondents reported using any pharmaceutical aid (ie, nicotine replacement product and/or an antidepressant). Use of pharmaceutical aids increased as the number of cigarettes per day increased.

No statistically significant differences were seen in mean NRT use over the three surveys—respondents remained on NRT a mean of 28.2 days in 1999 compared with 26.2 days in 1996 and 29.7 days in 1992. To some extent, duration of NRT use was related to payment modality. Some 39.5% of smokers with full insurance coverage of the NRT product used it for 6 weeks or longer. Of smokers with partial insurance coverage, 44.3% used the product for 6 weeks or longer. And, of smokers who incurred the full cost themselves, 21.8% used the product for 6 weeks or longer.

## Heaviest Smokers Show a Longer Time to Relapse

In the 1999 survey, slightly more than half of the NRT users (51%) used some type of behavior modification assistance, with the use of self-help materials selected as the assistance of choice (by 48.3%), followed by 9.3% for group counseling, and 7.5% for one-on-one counseling sessions.

Moderate-to-heavy smokers (defined as [greater than or equal to] 15 cigarettes a day) who used NRT in the 1992 and 1996 surveys experienced a statistically longer time to relapse than smokers who did not use a pharmaceutical aid to help quit smoking. However, in the 1999 survey, only about a 3 month advantage was seen for using NRT versus no pharmacologic aid among moderate-to-heavy smokers, according to a Cox proportional hazards regression analysis.

## Quitting Cold Turkey Works

For almost two decades the NRT [nicotine replacement therapy] industry blasted cold turkey quitting at every opportunity while using its economic muscle to erase abrupt nicotine cessation quitting recommendations around the globe. The industry made billions but when it came to quitting, recovered nicotine addicts were a bit smarter than the burning plant-matter between their lips made them appear.

Today 91.2% of all successful long-term quitters are quitting entirely on their own. Let me say that again, 91.2% of successful quitters did not purchase or use the nicotine patch, Zyban, nicotine gum, Wellbutrin, the nicotine lozenge, hypnosis, the nicotine spray, acupuncture, nicotine inhalers, magic herbs, laser therapy, or attend any formal quit smoking program. They did it entirely on their own!

John R. Polito, July 18, 2003. www.whyquit.com.

The researchers conclude that despite widespread promotion of pharmaceutical aids for smoking cessation throughout the 1990s, by 1999, the use of any pharmaceutical aid to quitting was low—around 17%. In 1999, although pharmaceutical aids collectively (ie, NRT and antidepressants) helped moderate-to-heavy smokers discontinue using cigarettes longer, they were not associated with a clinically meaningful long-term improvement in successful cessation and no benefit was observed in light smokers.

Having partial insurance coverage led to longer use, but only about 40% used NRT longer than the recommended minimum of 6 weeks. Yet insurance coverage cannot be the main reason for short duration of use—as mean duration of aid use was similar across all the surveys, which covered the time periods when these products were moved from "coverage product status" to over-the-counter status. The researchers attribute at least part of the high relapse rate to lack of adjuvant behavior counseling and lack of adherence to recommended guidelines on length of use of the NRT products.

*"School-based tobacco prevention programs . . . are most effective when the message is delivered repeatedly and is taken . . . seriously."*

# Government Programs Can Reduce Smoking

National Cancer Policy Board, Institute of Medicine, and National Research Council

*The National Cancer Policy Board, Institute of Medicine, and National Research Council are affiliated with the National Academy of Sciences, a private, nonprofit academy of scholars dedicated to the advancement of science and technology. In the following viewpoint, they argue that states that have implemented strong antismoking laws and regulations have shown a marked decrease in both teen and adult smoking. Other effective government initiatives include antismoking education programs and youth tobacco-access control laws, the authors contend.*

As you read, consider the following questions:

1. How many of the 1.8 million people who became daily smokers in 1996 were under age eighteen, according to the authors?
2. In the authors' view, by what percentage can school-based antismoking programs reduce smoking prevalence?
3. A cigarette price increase of 10 percent will reduce total consumption by what percent, according to most economists?

G rowing attention is focused on how states can prevent deaths due to tobacco use. Thus state governors, state legislators, and their staffs must decide whether to fund tobacco control programs, and, if they do, how much to spend on them.

The National Cancer Policy Board (a joint program of the Institute of Medicine and the National Research Council) is charged with carrying out policy analyses to help the nation deal with cancer; in 1997, it quickly identified tobacco's role as the foremost cause of cancer deaths as its first topic of concern. The board followed debates taking place in state capitals throughout 1998 and 1999, and decided in July 1999, in consultation with the Board on Health Promotion and Disease Prevention of the Institute of Medicine, that it would be useful to summarize evidence about the effectiveness of state tobacco control programs and to briefly describe those programs for state government officials.

Tobacco control will likely remain on the agenda of many states for several years. Public health advocates, tobacco firms, tobacco growers, retailers, and the general public have all been drawn into the debate. This report does not address the merit of tobacco control compared to alternative uses of state funds or attempt to balance the interests of contending stakeholders; instead, it focuses on the narrower question of whether state tobacco control programs can reduce smoking and save lives. As states contemplate increasing their tobacco control efforts, many have asked if such programs can make a difference. The evidence is clear: They can.

## High Stakes

Tobacco use kills more Americans each year than any other cause. The estimated 430,000 deaths attributed to tobacco use annually are far more than those caused by illegal drugs, homicides, suicides, AIDS, motor vehicle accidents, and alcohol combined. Lung cancer kills more Americans than breast and prostate cancer combined, and tobacco accounts for over 30% of all cancer deaths and a comparable fraction of deaths due to heart and lung diseases. Yet despite these risks, many, many people start smoking each year. In 1996, over 1.8 million people became daily smokers, two-thirds of them (1.2 million) under age 18.

Over the past decade, states have moved to the forefront of tobacco control. Starting with California in 1988, and followed by Massachusetts, Arizona, Oregon, and other states, referenda have increased tobacco excise taxes and dedicated a fraction of the revenues to reducing tobacco use. Legislatures in other states—such as Alaska, Hawaii, Maryland, Michigan, New Jersey, New York, and Washington—have increased tobacco taxes substantially, raising questions about how much of the revenue should go to tobacco control. In addition, settlements of lawsuits against tobacco firms to recoup state monies spent through Medicaid have now resulted in individual state revenue streams (in Florida, Minnesota, Mississippi, and Texas) or in revenues anticipated through the Master Settlement Agreement with the other states and territories signed in 1998. In aggregate, these agreements could transfer as much as $246 billion from tobacco firms to states over the next 25 years.

## The Evidence

The best evidence for the effectiveness of state tobacco control programs comes from comparing states with different intensities of tobacco control, as measured by funding levels and "aggressiveness." For example, when California and Massachusetts mounted programs that were more "intense" than those of other states, they showed greater decreases in tobacco use compared to states that were part of the American Stop Smoking Intervention Study (ASSIST) funded by the National Cancer Institute. From 1989 to 1993, when the Massachusetts program began, California had the largest and most aggressive tobacco control program in the nation, and it showed a singular decline in cigarette consumption that was over 50% faster than the national average. A recent evaluation of the Massachusetts tobacco control program showed a 15% decline in adult smoking—compared to very little change nationally—thus reducing the number of smokers there by 153,000 between 1993 and 1999. States that were part of the ASSIST program, in turn, devoted more resources to tobacco control than did other states except Massachusetts and California, and they showed in aggregate a

7% reduction in tobacco consumption per capita from 1993 to 1996 compared to non-ASSIST states. Such a "dose-response" effect is strong evidence that state programs have an impact, that more tobacco control correlates with less tobacco use, and that the reduction coincides with the intensification of tobacco control efforts.

A second line of evidence comes from observing effects on tobacco consumption beyond those associated with price. When tobacco prices rise, sales should drop, and when prices drop, sales should rise. Yet price alone does not explain the observed consumption patterns. In the first 2 years after Oregon's ballot initiative was implemented, for example, cigarette consumption dropped by over 11%, which is 5% more than would be expected from the price increase alone. The reported decreases in tobacco use in Alaska, California, and Florida similarly exceed what would be expected from price increases alone. Moreover, when cigarette prices dropped nationwide during 1992–1994, consumption rose in states with small tobacco control efforts but did not rise in 11 of 14 ASSIST states; consumption also plateaued in California and Massachusetts. This suggests that tobacco control measures limited the increase in tobacco sales expected as a result of a price drop.

In the review of tobacco control program elements that follows, results are reported in ranges, and sometimes those ranges are large. It is generally quite difficult to attribute a reduction in tobacco use to any single factor; often, many factors work in parallel. The underlying message is quite clear, however: Multifaceted state tobacco control programs are effective in reducing tobacco use.

## Counteradvertising and Education

Counteradvertising and public education campaigns have become standard elements of tobacco control, although their funding levels and aggressiveness vary considerably among the states. Counteradvertising campaigns can convey a variety of messages and can be aimed at different audiences. An evaluation of the California tobacco control program concluded that it was most effective in its early years, when the highest-impact advertisements emphasized deceptive practices undertaken by tobacco firms. Evaluators concluded that the program became less effective when spending for counteradvertising dropped (from $16 million in 1991 to $6.6 million by 1995), and when the advertisements began to focus on health risks rather than tobacco industry practices. As a result, the program's advisory committee made its foremost 1997 goal to "vigorously expose tobacco industry tactics." A "natural experiment" underway in Florida may provide further insight. The Florida Pilot Program, funded by that state's tobacco settlement, created the edgy "Truth Campaign" and SWAT (Students Working Against Tobacco) program. During its first year, tobacco use among youths decreased dramatically. The second-year budgets for both programs were seriously threatened in the Florida legislature—at one point facing extinction—but funding was partially restored. The program director was removed and the counteradvertising campaign was said to be heading "in a new direction." The budget for public media is slated to drop from $24 million to $18 million in the second year. If the rate of decline in tobacco consumption among youths stalls in Florida, as it did in California after 1994, this would provide further evidence that the "dose" of tobacco control predicts its impact.

School-based tobacco prevention programs are also part of state tobacco control programs. The effectiveness of school-based programs varies. They are most effective when the message is delivered repeatedly and is taken as seriously and promoted as powerfully as are other forms of drug abuse education. Properly implemented school programs can, however, lower smoking prevalence from 25% to 60%. These programs have been evaluated repeatedly, and in 1994 the Centers for Disease Control and Prevention (CDC) produced a set of guidelines for school-based programs. States will want to take care in implementing school-based programs, however, because they can consume considerable resources to little effect; a 1996 meta-analysis showed only a modest impact for most programs. The 1994 Institute of Medicine report *Growing Up Tobacco Free* noted the variable results of school-based programs but concluded that they should be part of a comprehensive tobacco control strategy because educating school-age children and adolescents about the consequences of tobacco use is clearly important to sustain a smoke-free norm.

Experimentation with the content and style of counteradvertising and education programs will and should continue, subject to evaluation to enable improvements and increase their impact. With that in mind, the American Legacy Foundation was established with funding from the 1998 Master Settlement Agreement. Its duties will include funding and oversight of a national counteradvertising campaign. Many states are also planning major increases in their counteradvertising and education initiatives.

## Smoke-Free Workplaces

The main impetus for smoke-free environments grew from concern about exposing nonsmokers to the toxic effects of tobacco smoke. Making worksites, schools, and homes smoke-free zones is a powerful strategy for reducing tobacco use overall because it boosts quit rates and reduces consumption. A 1996 review, for example, estimated that smoke-free workplaces reduced the number of smokers by 5% on average (meaning that almost one in five smokers quit, as smoking prevalence is about 25%) and reduced use among continuing smokers by 10%. Another review attributed over 22% of the tobacco consumption drop in Australia between 1988 and 1995, and almost 13% of the drop in the United States between 1988 and 1994, to smoke-free workplace policies. The death toll and ill-health attributable to involuntary smoking are thoroughly documented in a Surgeon General's report, a report from the federal Environmental Protection Agency (EPA), and a study by the California EPA. Federal regulations prohibit smoking in federal buildings and in airplanes. In some states and localities, laws and ordinances proscribe smoking in workplaces, schools, public spaces, restaurants, and other sites. Creating smoke-free workplaces and public spaces reduces tobacco use among smokers while reducing involuntary smoking by nonsmokers. Smoking restrictions have been a major focus of some states' tobacco control efforts and are a central thrust of much activity at the county and city levels.

# Taxation

Raising the price of tobacco products through taxation is one of the fastest and most effective ways to discourage children and youths from starting to smoke and to encourage smokers to quit. In 1994 and 1998, the Institute of Medicine recommended price increases of $2 per pack (or equivalent for other tobacco products), based on levels needed to approach the health goals in *Healthy People 2000* and to approach parity with other countries that have effective tobacco control programs. Wholesale prices have increased an average of $0.65 per pack nationwide since the Master Settlement Agreement was signed in 1998, the federal excise tax was raised to $0.24 per pack in the Balanced Budget Act of 1997, and six states now have excise taxes over $0.75 per pack. Even high-tax states remain short of the Institute's recommended level, however, and 20 states have excise taxes below $0.20 per pack. The wholesale price and excise tax increases do not necessarily imply equal increases in retail prices that consumers see, as discounts to retailers are commonplace for tobacco products, and local business factors are important. It is nonetheless clear that the floor for prices have risen, even if the ceiling is variable.

Economists have reached a consensus that a cigarette price increase of 10% will decrease total consumption by about 4%. Most economists now believe the response is larger (i.e., about 8%) among youths, based on recent studies. Conclusions about whether price disproportionately affects children and youths are based on fewer data than larger studies of total tobacco consumption. A classic 1990 study showed that responsiveness to price (elasticity of demand) increased over time from 1970 to 1985 but found little difference between adults and youths. A more recent review of more elaborate studies showed elasticities in the range noted above; it also found that youths were more sensitive to price, as demonstrated by fewer youths starting to smoke and reduced consumption among continuing youth smokers. An April 1998 report from the Congressional Budget Office reviewed many studies of price and consumption. It found unequivocal evidence that increased prices reduce use, although details about the mechanisms and effects are not completely understood. Proposals to increase cigarette taxes face strong opposition. (Interestingly, tobacco taxes are one of the few taxes for which a majority of Americans favor increases, especially if the revenues derived are dedicated to tobacco control.) The principal policy concern is that tobacco taxes are regressive, because tobacco use is more common among people with low incomes, and thus the poor spend proportionately more of their incomes on cigarettes. Tax increases are actually less regressive than simple projections suggest, however, because the poor are more sensitive to price and their consumption falls more sharply when prices rise. The World Bank supports increasing tobacco excise taxes for its public health impact and notes that judgments about regressiveness "should be over the distributional impact of the entire tax and expenditure system, and less on particular taxes in isolation."

Governors and legislators have raised concerns about increasing prices on tobacco because revenues from excise taxes might drop, along with payments expected under the Master Settlement Agreement (because payments to states are tied to sales). States concerned about revenue loss have an effective option—raising the state excise tax rate. The World Bank notes that "empirical evidence shows that raised tobacco taxes bring greater [overall] tobacco tax revenues." Reduced consumption will also ultimately lead to lower health costs to states through Medicaid and other health programs. In one study, the health benefits due to lower rates of heart attack and stroke began quickly, and the health benefits more than offset the program's cost after 1 year. The immediate economic and health benefits are later compounded by reductions in cancer and other chronic diseases.

**Treatment Programs**

Nicotine addiction, like other addictions, is a treatable condition. Treatment programs for tobacco dependence can work. States have two major roles in treating tobacco dependence: (1) educating tobacco-dependent people about their treatment options through public health programs, and (2) ensuring that medical programs cover and reimburse the costs of the treatments. As of 1997, only 22 states and the District of

Columbia covered such treatment under Medicaid, leading to a recommendation by D.C. Barker, C.T. Orleans, and H.H. Schauffler that state Medicaid agencies "incorporate explicit language into their managed-care contracts, policy briefs, lawsuit provisions, and Medicaid formularies." States can take guidance on policies to improve tobacco treatments from a report by the Center for the Advancement of Health.

Community-based resources such as centralized "quit-lines" and workplace wellness programs can increase access to cessation programs. State governments are among the largest employers in most states, and a major employer in all. States can ensure that their employees have access to treatment through their health plans, and smoking bans in state buildings can increase cessation and reduce tobacco use among continuing smokers. States can also pass laws to create smoke-free businesses, public buildings, and worksites. State and local media campaigns that reinforce nonsmoking norms also enhance motivation to quit, reduce tobacco use among those who continue to smoke, and prevent relapse.

Much can be done to improve access to and the effectiveness of treatment programs within medical systems. More than 70% of smokers visit a primary health care provider at least once a year. Systematic reviews conclude that routine, repeated advice and support can increase smoking cessation rates by 2- to 3-fold. Physicians, nurses, psychologists, dentists, and other health professionals are more likely to give such advice and support if they practice in a system that encourages such behavior through practice-based systems for tracking smoking status, office-based written materials for smokers to take home, training of health professionals in screening and advising patients, coverage of cessation programs by health plans, and reimbursement for treatments by payers (including Medicaid).

Most people who use tobacco—at all ages—express a desire to quit, but only a small fraction succeed on their own. Although many who do quit do so without formal treatment, treatment clearly improves cessation rates. Controlled studies generally report 30%–35% cessation rates at 1 year for intensive treatments and 10%–20% cessation rates for less-intensive treatments. Treatment for addiction to tobacco products ranks high in cost-effectiveness among health program spending options. Programs that combine behavioral therapies with pharmacotherapies (i.e., medications) have the best results, and evidence-based guidelines recommend that all smokers should be offered both. Behavioral programs can be delivered in group settings (in person) or individually (in person or by telephone). Food and Drug Administration (FDA)–approved medications include nicotine replacement agents (in gum, patch, nasal spray, or inhaler delivery systems) and the antidepressant drug bupropion.

Treatment works, but there is ample room for improvement. Despite evidence of its effectiveness, relatively few smokers seek out formal treatment, and relapse rates are high. Improving smoking cessation success rates would be especially important in certain target populations. For example, Massachusetts placed an emphasis on reducing smoking among pregnant women because it would produce long-lasting benefits for the prospective mothers and reduce risks to their children. As a result, the number of mothers who smoked during pregnancy dropped by almost 48% during 1990–1996, a rate far ahead that of any other state.

It has long been illegal—in every state—to sell tobacco products to minors, but until recently, enforcement was lax. The federal Synar Amendment ties federal block grant monies to improved compliance with state laws proscribing such sales. States risk reduced payments from the Substance Abuse and Mental Health Administration if they fail to meet compliance targets. The federal government has never withheld state funds based on the Synar Amendment, but such withholding is under discussion for several states that have not met Synar targets. Enforcement of youth sales, with mandatory ID-card inspection of those 26 and younger, was the central thrust of a 1996 FDA tobacco regulation. This part of the regulation remains in force pending a U.S. Supreme Court ruling about FDA's jurisdiction over tobacco products. States now have FDA contracts to enforce and monitor youth sales. Several reports have noted that enforcing laws against sales to minors can reduce tobacco consumption. Although one 1997 study of enforcement showed no decline in youth smoking, the authors attributed the lack of impact to insufficient merchant compliance and developed a model approach that is being used in Massachusetts. Excessive focus or exclusive reliance on youth access restrictions can siphon resources and political will from more powerful tobacco control measures. Yet all U.S. jurisdictions have youth access laws, and if those laws are to become meaningful, they must be enforced.

## Monitoring and Evaluating

Today's tobacco control programs build on decades of research and demonstrations. The scale and scope of tobacco control in the United States—particularly in the most aggressive states—has grown considerably over the past decade, and the proper balance and content of program elements are the subjects of continuing debate. Tobacco control can improve over time only if (a) its elements are assessed, (b) state programs that choose different strategies are compared, and (c) research to improve the programs is carried out. Governors and state legislators, moreover, need to be able to be accountable for the use of public dollars. This does not imply that results will be quick; significant reductions in tobacco use take years even in states where tobacco control has clearly been effective.

Performance monitoring of public health programs is receiving increased attention. Measures to monitor the performance of tobacco control programs are in place, and efforts are underway to improve them. Without specified goals and ways of measuring progress, the effectiveness of public monies spent on such programs is hard to judge, so state tobacco control programs should include resources for evaluation and research as part of a comprehensive tobacco control program.

# Periodical Bibliography

The following articles have been selected to supplement the diverse views presented in this chapter.

| *Chemist and Druggist* | "Hard Habit to Break," February 13, 1999. |
| David Cole | "Eateries Say Smoking Ban Hurts," *Journal Sentinel*, March 24, 2001. |
| Patrick Fleenor | "Cigarette Taxes, Black Markets and Crime: Lessons from New York's 50-Year Losing Battle," *Policy Analysis*, February 6, 2003. www.cato.org. |
| Karen Goldberg Goff | "Breaking the Chain of Smoking," *Washington Times*, October 8, 2000. |
| Wayne Hall | "The Prospects for Immunotherapy in Smoking Cessation," *Lancet*, October 5, 2002. |
| Prabhat Jha et al. | "Death and Taxes: Economics of Tobacco Control," *Finance and Development*, December 1999. |
| *Journal of Physical Education, Recreation and Dance* | "Higher Cigarette Taxes Curb Smoking," October 2001. |
| Sam Kazman | "Joe Camel Revisionism," *CEI Update*, February 1999. |
| *Medical Letter on the CDC and FDA* | "Cigarette Tax Hike Could Save Millions of Lives," September 22, 2002. |
| *Olympian* | "Our Views: Smoking Ban Impossible to Enforce," March 13, 2003. |
| John P. Pierce and Elizabeth A. Gilpin | "Impact of Over-the-Counter Sales on Effectiveness of Pharmaceutical Aids for Smoking Cessation," *Journal of the American Medical Association*, September 11, 2002. |
| John R. Polito | "JAMA Study Concludes NRT Is Ineffective," September 11, 2002. www.whyquit.com. |
| R. Emmett Tyrell Jr. | "Anti-Smoking Jihad in Montgomery County," *Conservative Chronicle*, December 12, 2001. |
| Lynne Wallis | "The Patch Test," *Nursing Standard*, March 12, 2003. |
| Elizabeth M. Whelan | "The U.S. Supreme Court Rejects FDA Tobacco Regulation: A Setback for Public Health?" March 22, 2000. www.acsh.org. |
| Mitchel L. Zoler | "Smoking Ban Cut MI Rates by 60%," *Cardiology News*, April 2003. |
| Nancy Zuckerbrod | "Panel Recommends FDA Regulation of Tobacco," *Detroit News*, January 27, 2001. |

# CHAPTER 4

# Is Tobacco Use a Serious Problem Worldwide?

# Chapter Preface

China, with a population of 1.23 billion people—about 20 percent of the world's total population—consumes 30 percent of the world's cigarettes. According to Zhang Yifang, vice president of the Chinese Association on Smoking and Health, the majority of smokers in his country are either unclear on the health effects of smoking or believe that it is good for them. He says, "They think it will increase their stamina, cure boredom, scare away insects and even prevent diseases as they get older. There's a popular saying that 'If you smoke and drink, you'll live to be 99.'"

Unfortunately, according to a study published in the *British Medical Journal* in 2001 that tracked the cause of death of over twenty-seven thousand men in Hong Kong, few Chinese smokers can look forward to a long and healthy life. Richard Peto, the Oxford University epidemiologist who led the study, maintains that "two-thirds of all the young men in China, but as yet, few of the young women, become smokers. . . . On present smoking patterns, about one-third of all the young men in China will eventually be killed by tobacco." Further, Peto and his colleagues contend that tobacco-related diseases kill about 1 million Chinese smokers each year. They predict that the number of smoking-related deaths will double by 2025 and reach 3 million per year by 2050 if the present trend is not reversed. China, with its huge population of smokers, widespread lack of accurate information about smoking, and high rate of tobacco-related fatalities, is just one example of the serious health problems that tobacco use causes worldwide.

The enormity of the smoking problem in China is exacerbated by the fact that the Chinese government—the world's largest producer of cigarettes—profits significantly from its tobacco industry and thus has a large economic stake in continued tobacco use. The government-owned State Tobacco Monopoly Administration, a network of plants responsible for processing and manufacturing 1.7 trillion cigarettes in 2001, makes most of the cigarettes the Chinese smoke. Cigarette production has doubled in the past twenty years, and now the Chinese government receives about 10 percent of its total tax revenue from the tobacco monopoly—about $14 billion in 2001. In addition, it is estimated that China has about 5 million tobacco farmers and that more than 100 million jobs overall are linked to growing, processing, manufacturing, and selling tobacco products.

The high rate of tobacco-related diseases and death in China is just one example of the problems caused by smoking. Authors in the following chapter explore other issues surrounding tobacco use around the world.

*"Within the next thirty years, tobacco is
likely to be the single biggest cause of death
worldwide, killing about 10 million
[people] per year."*

# Tobacco Use Is a Serious Problem Worldwide

Iraj Abedian

Tobacco use in developing countries has reached epidemic
proportions, causing an increase in tobacco-related diseases
and deaths worldwide, Iraj Abedian contends in the following
viewpoint. He argues that over eighty thousand young
people become addicted to tobacco each day and that the majority of them live in developing countries. Further, over the
next thirty years, tobacco use is likely to become the single
largest cause of death throughout the world. Iraj Abedian is a
professor of economics and director of the Applied Fiscal Research Center at the University of Cape Town, South Africa.

As you read, consider the following questions:

1. According to the author, what percentage of the world's
   smokers live in poorer nations?
2. What three internal factors does Iraj Abedian argue are
   responsible for the rise in smoking in developing
   countries?
3. In the author's opinion, how many people worldwide are
   addicted to smoking?

Iraj Abedian, address to the International Conference on Sustainable Structure
for Better Health, Budapest, Hungary, May 29–June 2, 2000. Copyright © 2000
by Iraj Abedian. Reproduced by permission.

Nowadays, it is beyond any doubt that smoking is a lethal habit. Even the tobacco industry no longer refutes the health hazards of smoking. Equally true is the fact that smoking is increasingly a developing country phenomenon. In terms of the 1996 statistics, the three countries of China, India and Indonesia alone consume 44% of the world tobacco. Over the past two decades the rapid rise in smoking prevalence among the poorer nations has increased their share of smokers to 70% of the total in the world. As importantly, the level of smoking, as measured by cigarettes per capita, has risen in the developing countries. Figure 1 below illustrates the overall pattern of per capita adult cigarette consumption in developed as well as developing countries.

## Smoking Is Increasing in the Developing World

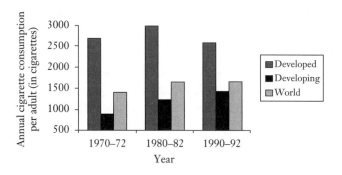

WHO (World Health Organization), 1997.

## Internal and External Factors

In response to nearly three decades of anti-tobacco public policies, the developed world is beginning to experience a decline in smoking prevalence. The public health consequences in these societies are thus likely to decrease accordingly. Meanwhile, the rise in smoking in the developing world may be attributed to two sets of internal and external factors. Chief amongst the internal factors are:

(a) *Illiteracy and Low Literacy:* It is generally recognised that consumer's knowledge is a key determinant of consumption

144

choice. Moreover, in the case of a hazardous item such as smoking, the level of literacy and education in general plays a major role in consumer choice. . . . To the extent that illiteracy, or literacy, is widespread in the developing countries, it predisposes the population to higher prevalence of smoking. Rising literacy on its own, however, does not guarantee lower consumption of tobacco. In fact, in many developing countries with rising literacy and higher income, smoking prevalence tends to increase. South East Asia over the 1980s and 1990s is a case in point. This is driven mostly by the 'income effect' and the 'impact of advertising'; in the absence of an effective public awareness programme. Low literacy, at the same time, undermines public health campaigns that rely on health warnings, and other forms of health education that require literacy.

(b) *Lack of public education and awareness:* Developing nations commonly lack adequate public health facilities and in general do not pay sufficient attention to preventive measures in the form of public education and awareness programmes. In the case of an addictive substance such as tobacco, this is a major drawback. The challenge is to avoid smoking habits to begin [with] and prevent addiction [from setting] in. Developing countries are generally least equipped to provide an effective and sustained public awareness programme. The population is thus left exposed to the health hazards of a variety of preventable diseases, including tobacco addiction.

(c) *Lack of political will:* Societal issues ultimately require political will to resolve. The public health hazards of smoking are no exception. Much too often the political leadership in the developing nations 'politick around' the health aspects of smoking as opposed to dealing with the hard choices that would provide effective solutions to the problem. One of the contributing factors in this regard is the short-term time horizon of political office bearers. Tobacco control policies pay off in the medium to long run. Meanwhile the politician's concern is mostly driven by short run prospects. In part this has to do with the issues of accountability and democratic governance as incorporated in the socio-political superstructure of the country. In some cases, lack of public resource availability is also a contributing factor. Whatever the cause roots of the phenomenon, the outcome is disastrous from a public health perspective.

## Global Factors Influence Smoking

Amongst the external, or global, factors that have raised the level of smoking in the developing world are the following:

i. *Rapid pace of Globalization:* Freer transfer of goods and easier availability of cigarettes have provided accessibility that did not exist before.

ii. *Trade Liberalisation and international Capital Flows:* Trade liberalisation has led to lower than otherwise prices for cigarettes. This in turn increases demand and consumption. Rising demand in the meantime provides the production scale that is needed for efficient local/regional manufacturing enterprises. Closely interrelated with this are the pressure for privatisation and the quest for foreign capital inflows. In a number of the developing countries, the manufacturing of cigarettes has been privatised, using foreign capital. This leads to a more efficient production, hence lowering of the price with a concomitant rise in consumption.

iii. *Lack of Co-ordination among Multilateral Institutions:* Historically, the tobacco policies of the multilateral institutions such as the WHO [World Health Organization], the UN [United Nations] agencies, the World Bank and the IMF [International Monetary Fund] have not been co-ordinated. This lack of policy co-ordination has in some instances led to contradictory policy prescriptions and investment strategies. Of late, however, there has been a rising level of co-operation among these institutions. In addition to the close collaboration between WHO and the World Bank, there is growing recognition that the UN agencies need to harmonise policies and practices if the massive global human losses of tobacco smoking are to be averted. To this end, the UN Economic and Social Council resolution 1999/56 of 30 July 1999 is a critical achievement. In terms of the resolution, a UN Ad Hoc Interagency Task Force is established as a focal point for global tobacco control. The WHO leads this task force. This augurs well for not only international policy co-ordination, but also for the success of the WHO's Tobacco Free Initiative.

iv. *Communication Revolution:* Unprecedented inventions and innovations in the communication technology has trans-nationalised, among others, cigarette advertising. National controls over the content and other aspects of advertising have diminished. As a result market penetration is made much easier and cheaper for the tobacco industry.

## Tobacco Use Has Reached Epidemic Proportions

The above list is by no means exhaustive. Yet it illustrates the fact that the combination of internal and external factors has created a global social milieu in which tobacco use has reached epidemic proportions. In terms of the most recent estimates:

- At present, over one billion people world-wide are addicted to smoking. This number is expected to rise to 1.6 billion over the next 25 years.
- Approximately 80,000 to 100,000 young people become addicted daily; the majority of these are in the developing countries.
- Within the next thirty years, tobacco is likely to be the single biggest cause of death worldwide, killing about 10 million per year. About half of these deaths will be in the working age of 35 to 69.
- It is estimated that about 500 million people alive today will eventually be killed by tobacco use. More than half of these will occur among today's children and teenagers.

The picture is particularly bleak for the developing countries. The estimated casualties of tobacco addiction are further compounded by the lack of social security systems, adequate public health facilities, and a pervasive general poverty. What these figures fail to show however, is the sheer magnitude of human sufferings that afflict not only the addicts themselves, but also their relatives and family members. It is the sum total of these personal and social costs that create a near catastrophic situation for the developing nations.

> *"It is impossible to quantify the contribution (if any at all) of tobacco in a death or disease."*

# The Problems Associated with Tobacco Use Worldwide Are Exaggerated

FORCES International

In the following viewpoint FORCES International claims that global public health agencies, such as the World Health Organization (WHO), purposely exaggerate the seriousness of worldwide tobacco use by inflating mortality rates and referring to tobacco use as an addiction or disease. FORCES International maintains that it is impossible to prove that tobacco use alone is responsible for death or disease anywhere in the world. FORCES International is a global organization of smokers and nonsmokers who believe that all people should be able to live free from excessive governmental and institutional interference.

As you read, consider the following questions:
1. According to the author, what is WHO's main accusation against the tobacco industry?
2. What does the author maintain will dramatically reduce the risks of smoking?
3. What is WHO's fundamental function, in the author's opinion?

FORCES International, "The Public Health Antismoking Scam: A Paper of Dissent," www.forces.org, December 2001. Copyright © 2001 by FORCES International. Reproduced by permission.

The most recent attack on private individuals and the tobacco industry by representatives of the World Health Organisation [WHO] is another demonstration of the fragility of their arguments. A close look at "Junking Science to Promote Tobacco" by Derek Yach and Stella Aguinaga Bialous (Derek Yach is with the World Health Organisation, Geneva, Switzerland. Stella Aguinaga Bialous is a public health policy consultant in San Francisco, Calif.) shows that the parameters of scientific, moral and political evaluation adopted by "public health" are the same distorted ones that the tobacco industry is accused of using.

The main accusation of the WHO and international public health against the tobacco industry is that the industry has distorted science to deflect the impact of primary and passive smoke on human health. Furthermore, the tobacco industry stands accused of hiring prominent scientists to question the validity of the assertions of "public health" (with the not-so-subtle implication that this amounts to scientific *corruption*). We neither dispute that experts have been hired by that industry to argue with the technicalities of "public health" assertions, nor do we dispute that such scientists have been paid fees for their consulting; that is, in fact, the normal way professionals earn their living.

That common practice, used by private industry to dispute and argue points of contention, should not be the concern of governments and of the citizens that they represent. Rather, the concern is that Public Health—an institution which, by definition, should be unbiased and solely concerned with policies based on solid scientific grounds—uses the *identical practices* of the tobacco industry, while pocketing lavish public funding. . . .

## Numbers Do Not Add Up

One of the tactics of the WHO in its effort to disinform governments and citizens about the health hazards of tobacco smoke is to mention mortality rates, and to project the use of tobacco as a social problem and a disease. *"Four million deaths per year, 1.2 billion smokers in the world today"*, Yach and Bialous flatly state. It is interesting to note that, according to the WHO's own 1997 World Health Report, the deaths were 3 million. A mere two years later, WHO's 1999 World Health Report states that there were 4 million deaths. That's an increase of 33% more dead smokers in only two years—a number they say that will increase to *10 million* in 19 years from now. To impress people more emphatically, predictions are based on predictions, which are based on estimates and projected estimates.

The statistical models used by the WHO are fundamentally flawed, and the methodology to enumerate the data is deeply corrupt. "Public health" is quick to dismiss as "tobacco paid" any opposition to what basically amounts to fraudulent information if the opposition comes from experts who have had any dealing whatsoever with the tobacco industry. On the other hand, independent, "non-expert" critiques, no matter how acute and to the point, are dismissed as incompetent, thus not worthy of attention. In fact, only antismoking activists and doctors—*doctors who embrace antitobacco*—are admitted to this exclusive "debate." This "debate," however, profoundly affects the pockets and the liberties of billions of smokers. Those smokers are expected to just blindly believe and obey public health's directives and accept its disinformation, without the opportunity, let alone the *right*, to have any say about policies and taxation launched against them.

## Non-Smokers Get the Same Diseases

However, it does not take a general practitioner to understand that all the diseases attributed to tobacco are multifactorial, often with hundreds—if not thousands—of concomitant causes which interact differently in every single human in function of hundreds of ever-changing variables. Another complication is that *all* the diseases attributed to tobacco also occur in non-smokers. It is therefore clear that it is *impossible* for multifactorial epidemiology to confidently isolate single co-factors such as primary or passive tobacco smoke exposure; thus, it is impossible to quantify the contribution (if any at all) of tobacco in a death or disease. From that fundamental concept alone it follows that the WHO's figures concerning tobacco-related mortality and morbidity are *invalid* as policy-making tools, and can only be relegated to the role—if any—of a rough indicator for speculative assumptions and/or further investigation. That is because those figures are based on *impossible quantification*—although a very complex, abstract, and highly technical set of parameters, methodologies, assumptions and terminology are used to impress unskilled media and political targets. This is done to project the impression of a highly sophisticated (thus *reliable*) statistical technology, which is then presented by doctors and academicians to add the essential ingredient of credibility to the antismoking saga. Governments and institutions are then induced, in turn, to move legally and politically against the tobacco industry and its 1.2 billion customers. But there is no magic in multifactorial epidemiology: beyond the smoke-screen, the WHO cannot prove, even for one single subject, that a direct cause-effect relationship (that is, *single etiological causality*) exists beyond any reasonable doubt. Yet, Yach states: *"The causal relationship between tobacco use and death and disease has been demonstrated in countless epidemiological studies over the last 50 years."* Projecting absolute certainty, without the humility and the doubt that good science always expresses, is one of the well established strategies of "modern public health."

In simple words, let us consider the enormous magnitude of the WHO's claims: four million-plus deaths per year "attributed" to smoking. With such a massive background of "fatalities," there should be no problem at all in presenting one single death that can be proven to be caused uniquely by primary or passive smoking, and beyond any scientific objection. At least, the WHO should be able to firmly quantify the percentage contribution of tobacco to that one death. But in no case can the WHO, or any other entity or individual, make such a claim; and if all the apocalyptic documentation of the WHO is read analytically, one sees that that claim is made nowhere.

## The "Safer Cigarette" Solution

Ironically, the same "public health" establishment that claims that so much death and disease is caused by primary and passive smoke wilfully ignores or smears any alternative in connection with smoking other than the unrealistic, and at any rate very long term, total elimination of smoking. Yet antismoking "education" is a credible cause of the dramatic increase in youth smoking, for which tobacco advertisement is instead blamed, even in those countries (such as Italy) where it has been forbidden for nearly four decades.

## Misrepresention of Tobacco Facts

When confronted with the scientific uncertainty, the inconsistency of results and the incredible misrepresentation of present-day knowledge, those seeking to abolish tobacco invoke a radical interpretation of the Precautionary Principle: "Where potential adverse effects are not fully understood, the activity should not proceed." . . .

If we continue down this dangerous path of control and prohibition based on an unreliable or remote chance of harm, how many personal freedoms will remain seven generations from now?

Eric Boyd, *The Record*, November 20, 2002.

For some time, the technology has existed to dramatically reduce the risks of smoking—no matter how unquantifiable, and whatever those risks may be—without depriving smokers of their lifestyle preference. The so-called "safer cigarette," based on halving the amount of untreated tobacco (thus halving pollutants in primary and passive smoke) and increasing the nicotine concentration (whose positive effects on health are widely recognised to the point that the pharmaceutical industry attempts to seize the control of it) has been available for many years, and its merits, even recently, have been independently recognised. The high concentration of nicotine augments the smoker's feeling of satisfaction, and further reduces the number of cigarettes smoked. But since its inception, the "safer cigarette" has been ignored or even fiercely opposed by the very establishment that often defines cigarette smoking as the "greatest man-made source of preventable disease."

In fact, the science and technology asserting that safer (more properly: less-hazardous) cigarettes were possible goes back to the Smoking and Health Program of the US National Cancer Institute, a program held jointly with the co-operation of the tobacco industry. Information about this program and the technology resulting from the research was initially made public through the efforts of Dr. James Watson, of DNA and Nobel prize fame. The opposition to a safer cigarette began in 1978 in the US. In 2001 the Institute of Medicine of the US National Academy of Sciences has confirmed that the suppressed 1980 policies for safer cigarettes were sound. It follows that, with its opposition, "public health" by its own count may be responsible for untold millions of premature deaths and avoidable diseases worldwide. . . .

## Ethical Considerations

The concept of a world free of hunger and disease is noble and desirable and, although we are still far away from that accomplishment, we must always tend to the achievement of that goal. Quality of life, however, is not measured only in terms of clinical health. Many believe that a long, healthy life achieved at the price of brutal enforcement, regulation, suppression of pleasure—not to mention the social cost of corrupting institutions and negating liberties and personal choice—is not worth living. That basic view, however, seems to elude the WHO and "public health" completely, as what they are doing is an absolute antithesis of everything a free civilised society stands for, and is ominously reminiscent of the darkest hours of the USSR.

The "new approach" and tactics of the WHO, and "public health" in general, brings forward disturbing considerations with respect to the role of health authorities—especially in times of advancing globalisation. An international authority concerned with threatening menaces such as malaria or the communicable disease AIDS, is desirable and indispensable. But the over-expansion of that authority for the imposition of "healthy" lifestyles on the global population is another matter altogether. For one thing, responding to the challenge of conventional health emergencies is very different from taking on the project of coercing disease prevention and maximising healthy life styles. Permitting the WHO, or any government, to proceed too far down the latter road poses serious questions for any society that wishes to be liberal and democratic.

## Meddling in Internal Policies

By going down this road the WHO is beginning to meddle in internal policies of countries, to interfere with economics, commerce and advertising, and even presumes to influence moral and ethical values. If this does not overstep the WHO's moral and functional limits, it should. Furthermore, the adoption of intimidation, political arm-twisting, and the systematic use of disinformation and junk science to push the WHO's agenda is unworthy of its purpose, and is deeply debilitating to the credibility of science in general, and medicine in particular. Finally, and perhaps more importantly, the blatant conflict of interest between the World Health Organisation (and "public health" in general) and the pharmaceutical multinationals should be examined very closely—and dramatically uprooted. Nowhere is that conflict more strikingly visible than in tobacco control.

"Tobacco control" uses international treaties to undermine the sovereignty of individual nations so that its interests can create public policy with a fait accompli on a global scale. The menace that this initiative creates for the sovereignty of nations cannot be overemphasised: the tobacco control treaty forces nations to open their doors to the special interests of the pharmaceutical industry through a channel that is not the normal marketplace. At the same time, it sets into place the precedent of a undemocratic supranational governing mechanism for health policy within nations. The pharmaceutical industry, which is rapidly consolidating and striving to realise the remarkable potential of contemporary biotechnology, may well be the most powerful industry in the world. That an international organisation supposedly representing the world's peoples should see itself in partnership with such an industry, is cause for concern.

## WHO Promotes Pharmaceuticals

In the tobacco control field, for all intents and purposes, the WHO has become the legitimising enabler of the marketing programs of the pharmaceutical multinationals:

• It ignores or discredits its own scientific evidence when it does not produce the desired antismoking results.

• It openly undermines the tobacco industry, facilitating

the pharmaceutical industry's control of the nicotine market.

• It accepts funds and resources from pharmaceutical conglomerates, to the point of becoming their "official partner".

• It promotes and supports pharmaceutically-funded antitobacco "studies" designed to further its antismoking agenda, while consciously ignoring the vast amount of scientific evidence that disputes, does not corroborate, or even exonerates tobacco from unprovable allegations against it.

• It pushes pharmaceutical smoking cessation products with a zeal unmatched by the best, for-hire marketing companies.

• It wilfully promotes intolerance by instigating nonsmokers against smokers. The social hostility that is created is apparently designed to intimidate smokers, and in this it largely succeeds, with devastating long-term social effects.

• It interferes with the cultural and democratic processes of nations in order to instigate smoking bans, and to induce smokers to purchase the products of its "benefactors" to socially "fit in."

• It interferes with the internal public health/socialised medicine of nations, pushing to change public health priorities, and to include cessation products that are either 80–85% defective, don't work at all—or may be deadly—in statesubsidised drug programs, thus affecting the distribution of the resources allocated for essential drugs. . . .

## Compassionate Relief

We need, in short, to return the WHO to its fundamental function: the compassionate relief from the pain and suffering of the human condition through research and help. We need to irreversibly immunise the WHO from politics and corporate involvement, impose public transparency and scrutiny on its agendas and scientific databases, and to dramatically resize the bureaucratic monster it has become—a machine that eats up 75% of its budget in "administrative overheads." It is also indispensable, before any other consideration, to focus its range of interests and authority directly to basic and devastating diseases that are tangibly quantifiable without abstruse and questionable computer programs and methodologies.

*"There are . . . a number of clear examples where the harmful impact of globalization on health is irrefutable. One . . . is the deadly global reach of the tobacco industry."*

# Globalization Contributes to Harmful Tobacco Use Worldwide

David Werner

David Werner argues in the following viewpoint that if current globalized trade policies are not changed, smoking will become one of the most significant causes of death in the world. He maintains that the greatest increase in tobacco-related deaths will take place in China, where tobacco taxes are the single largest source of government revenue. The work of nongovernmental agencies (NGOs), Werner insists, is critical to the worldwide economic reform that will stop the global epidemic of tobacco use. David Werner is an international health care activist and a founding member of the International People's Health Council.

As you read, consider the following questions:

1. According to the author, how many smoking-related deaths will occur annually by the year 2020?
2. Why is China's entry into the World Trade Organization likely to cause a drastic increase in tobacco use in China, in Werner's opinion?
3. What does Werner argue is the first step to reforming the unhealthy and unfair aspects of the global free-market system?

David Werner, "Evidence of Globalization's Negative Impact on Health: The Smoking Gun," www.politicsofhealth.org, September 15, 2003. Copyright © 2003 by Healthwrights. Reproduced by permission.

The impact of economic globalization on the current and long-term well being of humanity has been much debated. Those who proclaim the benefits of globalization—and even those who are trying to objectively understand its pros and the cons—often complain that much of the vehement protest against globalization, though full of sound and fury, is rhetorical and lacks solid evidence. Unfortunately, this is too often the case.

There are, however, a number of clear examples where the harmful impact of globalization on health is irrefutable. One of the most blatant examples, where a "smoking gun" is plainly evident, is the deadly global reach of the tobacco industry.

According to the World Health Organization (WHO), tobacco smoking is fast becoming one of the biggest health problems of our times. While consumption of cigarettes has diminished somewhat in the United States and (to a lesser extent) in Europe due to public education about its harm, in much of the world tobacco use is increasing. This is especially true in underdeveloped countries and Eastern Europe, where the multinational tobacco companies have intensified their marketing.

The WHO states that smoking has become one of the biggest causes of death in the world. It estimates that if current policies of globalized trade remain unaltered, by the year 2020 tobacco will contribute to over 10 million deaths annually.

## Deaths from Smoking Will Increase

The biggest increase in deaths from smoking, says WHO, will take place in China. Smoking has long been a serious health problem in China. It increased drastically following the Chinese Revolution, partly due to the widespread image of Chairman Mao, who was a chain smoker.

In the mid-1990s, Dr. Carl Taylor, working with the United National Children's Fund [UNICEF], helped to coordinate a nation-wide survey which showed that 60 percent of men in China smoked. By contrast, only 4 percent of women were smokers. This survey was conducted by the Chinese health ministry in preparation for a worldwide conference on

Smoking and Health, held in China in 1998. Since that occasion, with new awareness of the huge health and medical costs of smoking, the Chinese Health Ministry has made a concerted effort to try to reduce tobacco use among its citizens. But it has been an uphill battle.

The primary problem has been the powerful leverage of the multinational tobacco industry, coupled with conflicts of interest within the Chinese government itself. The multinational tobacco companies, especially those based in [the] United States, have targeted China—the world's most populous nation with over one billion people—as potentially their fastest-growing market. Because relatively few Chinese women smoke, the main target of their advertising and promotion will be young women, along with adolescents of both sexes. To hook the women, the industry will promote brands—such as "Virginia Slims"—as a status symbol of the modern, sexy, liberated woman. With such seductive marketing, the corporations are confident they can snare literally millions of women. For many they are fully aware that this will be a death sentence. But business is business.

## Import and Export of Tobacco Is Forbidden

China's Health Ministry has made efforts to slow down this trend. Recently it has passed laws to prohibit smoking in public places. (These laws are still not well enforced). The Ministry has advocated prohibiting both the import and advertising of foreign tobacco products. But because of the big stick of [the] globalized market system, such regulations cannot be approved.

A complicating factor is China's plan to become a member of the World Trade Organization [WTO]. In order to sustain its current double-figure rate of economic growth, the government considers it imperative to join the WTO. But to do so, China will be compelled to comply with WTO's trade liberalization requirements, including deregulation of the import and advertising of tobacco. In short, Marlboro and other multinationals will be given a free hand to bombard China with their carcinogenic products and promote them through multimillion-dollar advertising campaigns.

Another complicating factor is that many Chinese economists are not eager to see a reduction in tobacco consumption. This is because in China—as in many other countries—the biggest source of government revenue is the tobacco tax. To compensate, the health ministry has proposed a steep increase in the federal tobacco tax. Studies in several countries have shown that when the tobacco tax is increased, cigarette consumption declines. If the Chinese tobacco tax is doubled, the number of cigarettes smoked will predictably drop by half. Yet revenue from tobacco would stay much the same.

## The Tobacco Tax

Clearly, an increase in the tobacco tax would make sense from both an economical and a health point of view. But not from the viewpoint of the tobacco companies. Along with other giant industries, the tobacco industry has a strong influence on global trade agreements. Consequently, one of the conditions for China's entry into the WTO is that the current tobacco tax be cut in half. This combined with the import and aggressive marketing of Western brand-name cigarettes is certain to cause a drastic increase in tobacco consumption and its costly consequences, with no corresponding increase in government revenue.

The cards are stacked for a major, though potentially preventable, health disaster. China's compliance with the WTO requirements is predicted to increase by many millions the number of tobacco-related deaths, especially of women. But for China to integrate more fully into the global economy, a massive human sacrifice—comparable to the Holocaust in both numbers and twisted values—seems unavoidable. The world's most populous nation is well on the way to becoming yet another pawn in the inequitable global system.

## Changing the Globalized System

Can such a massive human sacrifice to the juggernaut of free-market development be avoided? Not easily. To avoid it will require a sweeping transformation of the dominant globalized economic system. This will be difficult because the world's economic and trade policies are dictated, undemocratically and often behind closed doors, by an elite minority with enormous power and wealth. As can be seen by the murderous invasion of the transnational tobacco industry into China, we do indeed live in an age "when corporations rule the world." And the corporate development model of lop-sided economic growth regardless of the human and environmental costs is not only ruthlessly widening the gap between rich and poor and endangering the health of millions of people. It is unbalancing vital ecological systems and endangering the continuity of life on this planet.

## China's Smokers

China, with a population of 1.23 billion people, has more than 320 million smokers. Two-thirds of Chinese men smoke, and they often offer cigarettes as greetings when meeting friends or strangers. Fewer Chinese women smoke, but cigarette smoking is a habit that spans all social and economic categories. . . .

With about one-fifth of the world's population, China consumes nearly one-third of the world's cigarettes. Most of those are produced by the State Tobacco Monopoly Administration, a vast network of government-owned processing and manufacturing entities that last year put 1.7 trillion cigarettes on the market.

Michael Dorgan, Knight-Ridder Washington Bureau, July 10, 2002.

For those of us who are committed to working toward the building of healthy communities for a sustainable future, action at the local level is essential but not enough. In the long-term view of things, if our local advances are not to be swept aside by global events (e.g., global warming) we must also concern ourselves actively with the global efforts to reform and eventually transform the current inequitable and unsustainable model of "development" at the global level (of which the WTO-condoned tobacco invasion of China is but one example).

The first step in working toward reforming the unhealthy and unfair aspects of the global free-market system—and eventually transforming that system into one that is equitable and sustainable—is for more people to become better informed. More people, at very societal level, need to understand how macro-economic policies affect their daily lives and endanger the future of their children. They need to perceive the shortsighted, undemocratic power plays that put those unfair and unhealthy policies into place. They need the analytic skills to comprehend the way corporate dollars have purchased public elections, undermined democratic process, and put the economic growth of the wealthy before the wellbeing of people and the environment. And with this new understanding, better-informed people around the world can join together to have a stronger voice in the decisions and regulations (or deregulations) that affect their lives. They can begin to mobilize, and eventually elect officials that put healthy and sustainable wellbeing of people and planet before the greed-driven development paradigm imposed on the world by the privileged few.

## NGOs Must Help

Such an awakening to the realities of our time by a critical number of the world's people will require a huge and coordinated effort. The challenge is made mere daunting by the fact that the mass media (mainstream newspapers, TV, etc.) are controlled by the same economic giants—the arms, oil, pharmaceuticals, alcohol, tobacco, and other industries—that control the global marketplace. Therefore it is essential that progressive NGOs (nongovernmental agencies) committed to a livable future make a concerted effort—in addition to their local health end development initiatives—to raise awareness about the global obstacles facing humanity and the planet, and to help to build coalitions for change at the macro level.

Unless our immediate efforts to enable marginalized peoples or conserve endangered ecosystems at the local level go hand-in-hand with a long-term strategy to transform our dangerously inequitable and unsustainable global market system, all our local endeavors are likely to come to naught. It is no longer enough to "think globally and act locally." To advance toward change for a livable future we must "think and act both locally and globally."

Local empowerment and action is still the heart of equitable and sustainable development. And helping people find ways to cope with hunger, poverty, and unfair social structures must necessarily come before more long-term strategies to reform and eventually transform the unfair structures themselves. But today more than ever we must not lose sight of the forest for the trees. As we plan and evaluate coping strategies at the local level, we must repeatedly ask ourselves, "to what extent do our local activities sow the seeds or help prepare the way for building healthier, more sustainable structures and policies at the national and international level." Without far-reaching change at the macro level, the changes we work so hard for at the local level are increasingly less likely to survive. We cannot seriously talk about sustainable change at the community level, without pursuing change at the global level.

*"Many of the print ads for tobacco in Asia
feature Western women who espouse ideals
of empowerment, individuality, and
rebellion."*

# Tobacco Advertising Is Encouraging Women Throughout the World to Smoke

Noy Thrupkaew

Declining profits due to tobacco lawsuits in the United States lawsuits and antismoking campaigns have prompted U.S. tobacco companies to look to women in developing nations as a new market, Noy Thrupkaew argues in the following viewpoint. Thrupkaew maintains that Asian women in particular, who usually smoke far less than Asian men, represent an untapped market. Cigarette advertising directed at women in developing countries encourage women to see smoking as a way to exert their independence, Thrupkaew asserts. Noy Thrupkaew is a freelance writer based in the Washington, D.C. area.

As you read, consider the following questions:
1. According to the author, how much have Philip Morris's overseas profits increased in the last ten years?
2. What are the five top cigarette markets worldwide, in Thrupkaew's opinion?
3. In the author's view, how are cigarette companies telling women abroad to resolve the conflict between ethnic heritage and "Americanization"?

Noy Thrupkaew, "The New Face of Tobacco: Women," *Z Magazine*, February 14, 2001. Copyright © 2001 by Z Magazine. Reproduced by permission of the author.

W hile the Marlboro Man surveys the great Eastern frontier from posters, walls, and cigarette stands all over Vietnam, young "Marlboro cowgirls" offer free cigarettes to pedestrians and beckon young people into company-sponsored events such as "Hollywood Nite."

In Japan, ad copy for Virginia Slims cigarettes—the most popular women's brand in the world—reads, "I'm going the right way—keeping the rule of the society, but at the same time I am honest with my own feeling. So I don't care if I behave against the so-called 'rules' as long as I really want to." In the background, a slim woman with indeterminate facial features—the glamorous, possibly Asian, possibly Caucasian kind of face that dominates the media in many Asian countries—embraces a fair-haired man. The tag line for this campaign? "Be You."

Meanwhile, in the United States, Philip Morris donates money to domestic violence shelters in communities of color; and sponsors minority women's groups such as the Mexican American National Women's Association. And in their most recent move to target U.S. women of color, Philip Morris launched a $40 million "multicultural" ad campaign for their Virginia Slims cigarettes in December 1999 that featured Asian, African, Latina, and white models under the slogan, "Find Your Voice."

What's behind these campaigns? According to tobacco-control activists, recent slow profits and damaging lawsuits against big tobacco in the United States have resulted in an onslaught of marketing dollars directed at these two untapped markets: women overseas, particularly women living in developing nations, and minority women in the United States.

U.S.-based transnational tobacco corporations such as Philip Morris, which owns both Marlboro and Virginia Slims, suffered several highly publicized setbacks within the past two years [1998–2000], including the 1998 Master Settlement Agreement (MSA). The settlement banned outdoor advertising and the use of cartoons in advertising cigarettes, and prohibits the targeting of youth—a major tobacco market—in promotions, advertising, or marketing. As a result, the overseas market has become even more appealing to the tobacco industry. "As the United States has been clamping down on [the tobacco industry], the money they put abroad has been increasing exponentially," said Joon-Ho Yu, program coordinator for the California-based Asian and Pacific Islander American Health Forum (APIAHF), one of four groups in the California Joint Ethnic Tobacco Education Networks.

## Overseas Profits Increase

U.S. tobacco companies have seen huge results from their overseas campaigns, which more than compensate for slower profit increases in the United States. In contrast to declining smoking rates in industrialized countries, smoking in developing nations has skyrocketed in the past twenty years. Philip Morris, the world's largest cigarette company, raked in huge profits from its international marketing—overseas profits soared 256 percent in the last ten years [1990–2000], while profits in the United States increased only 16 percent.

Alarmed by statistics on rising rates of smoking in developing nations, public health officials and tobacco activists in 1996 began to formulate an international treaty on tobacco control that would set legally binding global standards on tobacco-control issues, including advertising, taxation, and education and prevention. Since that time, the World Health Organization (WHO) Framework Convention for Tobacco Control (FCTC) has gained momentum—if ratified by all 191 member nations, the convention could put a serious dent in transnational tobacco's grip on markets overseas. As for tobacco's strategies in this country, the "Find Your Voice" campaign is just the latest sign that in the United States, the "next great frontier" for the tobacco industry is women of color, according to Alvina Bey Bennett, the chair of Virginia's National Coalition FOR Women AGAINST Tobacco.

According to Gregory Connolly, director of the Massachusetts Tobacco Control Program, "Since the Master Settlement Agreement, there has been a very sharp increase of cigarette advertising directed toward ethnic females. There's been a change and shift in the types of models in the ads—Virginia Slims went from using whites to a 'rainbow' strategy [in the "Find Your Voice" ads] as a way to pay the bill."

## Counter-Campaigns Emerge

In the United States, work on the development of "Find Your Voice" counter-campaigns has galvanized women's tobacco-control groups. The National Coalition FOR Women AGAINST Tobacco launched their "Loud and Clear" campaign in response to the "Find Your Voice" ads, creating educational counter-ads and action kits for women's and girls' organizations across the country. The Women's Tobacco Control Coalition awarded over $40,000 in grants to Los Angeles community organizations to curb smoking among young women and girls of color.

For many U.S. tobacco-control activists, the increased domestic marketing directed at minority women is inextricably linked to the targeting of women overseas. According to Bennett, "Everybody wants to mimic American life, it's a good life. If inequalities dominate your day-to-day life, escaping with a cigarette is very appealing. The same applies to minority women. Despite the wonderful standard of living in this country, there are pockets of poverty and lower levels of education, and ethnic groups are prey to the selling of the myth of freedom and glamour and wealth through cigarettes." In addition, armed with the knowledge that "when [U.S. anti-tobacco activists] make a dent here, [tobacco responds by] becoming rampant globally," according to Yu, women tobacco activists in the United States are focusing their energies on both domestic and international campaigns. "After all," said Bonnie Kantor, the network manager of the U.S.-based International Network of Women Against Tobacco, "if [the tobacco industry] can't do it here, we have to make sure they can't do it over there."

## The Tobacco Empire Expands

The tobacco industry has already gained a strong foothold in the male market. The majority of men in China, the United States, Japan, Russia, and Indonesia—the top five cigarette markets worldwide in 1996—called themselves smokers.

Women in these countries, however, have a much lower level of smoking. In Vietnam, the country with the highest smoking prevalence in the world, 74 percent of men smoke, compared to a mere 4 percent of Vietnamese women. These low numbers among women, according to tobacco-control activists, could mean big dollars to U.S.-based transnational corporations. Patti Lynn, the associate campaign director of the corporate accountability organization INFACT noted, "In developing countries, the women have often traditionally not smoked and represent an incredibly lucrative expansion market for U.S.-based transnational corporations."

## Women Are a Prime Target

As part of their strategy to encourage women to smoke, the tobacco industry first distinguished women from the larger body of current and future smokers. The *Tobacco Reporter*, a tobacco industry trade journal, summarized the corporate sentiment as,

> Women smokers are likely to increase as a percentage of the total. Women are adopting more dominant roles in society: they have increased spending power, they live longer than men. And as a recent official report showed, they seem to be less influenced by the anti-smoking campaigns than their male counterparts. All in all, that makes women a prime target as far as . . . any alert marketing man is concerned.

Katharine Doland et al., *Journal of the American Medical Women's Association*, Fall 2000.

As a result, "transnational tobacco companies have shifted their focus to developing nations with aggressive marketing campaigns targeting women and girls," according to a WHO report. The development of "women's brands" featuring "light" or "slim" cigarettes, the barrage of goods such as hats, lighters, skirts, and purses covered with tobacco logos, the sponsorship of disco dances and beauty pageants, and the use of women as "cigarette girls" to give away free samples are some of the tactics used by tobacco companies to entice women to smoke.

Much of the attention is focused on Asia, with its enormous potential markets of China and Southeast Asia and just-developing free-market systems, where the enforcement of trade regulations is not always consistent. This laxity produces what Soon-Young Yoon, New York liaison between WHO and the Campaign for Tobacco-Free Kids, called a marketing "free for all" that results in rising rates of smoking. WHO predicted that sales in Asia would increase by 35 percent by 2000, and tobacco companies are spending advertising dollars to ensure that Asian women will be part of the next wave of smokers. Many of the print ads for tobacco in Asia feature Western women who espouse ideals of empowerment, individuality, and rebellion.

## White Models Sell More Cigarettes

Japan's largest advertising agency, Dentsu, asserts that white models lend a "sense of foreignness to Japanese products, serving as symbols of prestige, quality, and modernity. . . . In the globalized context of consumer culture, a Western woman and her choice of cigarettes project a powerful symbol," according to a WHO report entitled "The Culture of the Body."

In response to international marketing strategies, feminist activists working on the Framework Convention on Tobacco Control have pushed for bans on advertising and the printing of tobacco logos on high-products, in addition to urging the tobacco-control movement to become more inclusive of women. Soon-Young Yoon explained, "We are not just victims of advertising, but need to be seen as leaders in the tobacco control movement."

That idea rings true to tobacco activists in the United States who are working to empower women in their own communities, especially as U.S. tobacco activists have started to recognize the repercussions of gains made in the United States on the developing world. "Tobacco control is like a water balloon," said Kantor, "you push it down here and it bulges out there."

Recognition of this permeability between communities in the United States and those abroad has shed new light on the importance of minority women to the tobacco industry, according to some tobacco activists. "The women in other countries tend to look up to American women as being more successful and leading more exciting lives. And anyone who can fly back to their homeland, or their parents' homeland—such a person would be locked up to," explained John Banzhaf of ASH. "In a sense, that woman who returns becomes a walking advertisement, a billboard for not just smoking but for a specific product."

## Traditional Women Are the Target

Recognizing the transnational nature of growing segments of the U.S. population, tobacco-control activists became alarmed when the Virginia Slims "Find Your Voice" ads first appeared in a September 1999 *Advertising Age* article on the new campaign. The ads, which have several different permutations, often feature women in traditional clothing, and have copy in languages such as Swahili and Spanish. Officially released in November 1999, the ads appeared in magazines such as *Glamour, Ladies' Home Journal, People, Essence, Vibe, Black Elegance*, and *Latina*.

The ads "signaled to me that the industry was going to use a more far-reaching approach in their recruitment of women here and abroad," said National Coalition FOR Women AGAINST Tobacco Chair Bennett. Filled with exotic images of "foreign-ness"—different languages, kente cloth, an African woman in a headwrap, an Asian woman with heavy face paint and silk robes, and stereotypical messages (for the Asian woman, "In silence I see, with wisdom I speak")—the ads present the flip side of most of the advertising in Asia, which peddles an equally exotic Westernization. With the "Find Your Voice" ads, Virginia Slims manages to sell a message of seeming tolerance (for international women of color in stereotypical roles) to a white audience, and acceptance for the ethnic heritage of minority women (as long as they adopt the Western method of "finding their voice" by lighting up).

And the "Find Your Voice" ads can exert a powerful pull, according to Bennett. "They are telling women you can become acculturated, but can maintain that part of your heritage. And it's working. It's not okay for Asian American women to smoke, but in this ad, they're telling you that you can retain 'traditional' elements of your heritage even though you smoke. For African American women who are searching for that identity and link with their heritage, the message 'No single institution owns the copyright to beauty' next to a beautiful African woman—that's powerful." The same could be said about women abroad, who are continually bombarded with images of "Western" lifestyles, attitudes, and bodies that are too often contrasted against and privileged above their own. So for U.S. women of color and women abroad, what's the way to solve any tension between an ethnic heritage and "Americanization," between being a non-Western woman and desiring goods and attitudes the tobacco industry has forcibly equated with Westernization? Just smoke a cigarette.

# Periodical Bibliography

The following articles have been selected to supplement the diverse views presented in this chapter.

Kweku Afriyie — "Speech Delivered at the Third Afro Meeting for Tobacco Control in Abidjan, Ghana," February 27, 2002. www.cdc.gov.

George A.O. Alleyne — "World No Tobacco Day," Pan American Health Organization, May 31, 2000. www.paho.org.

Susan Batchelor — "Traditional Women Are Tobacco's New Global Market," *Tobacco Week News*, August 8, 2003. www.tobaccowars.com.

Eric Boyd — "The Risks of Smoking Are Greatly Exaggerated," *Record*, November 20, 2002. www.freerepublic.com.

Center for Communications, Health and the Environment — "Women, Girls and Tobacco: An Appeal for Global Action," July 6, 2002. www.ceche.org.

Centers for Disease Control and Prevention — "Global Tobacco Prevention and Control: An Overview," April 24, 2003. www.cdc.gov.

Centers for Disease Control and Prevention — "Youth Tobacco Use and Exposure Is a Global Problem," August 28, 2002. www.cdc.gov.

Marianne C. Delpo — "Tobacco Abroad: Legal and Ethical Implications of Marketing Dangerous United States Products Overseas," *Business and Society Review*, Summer 1999.

Michael Dorgan — "Marlboro Man Would Feel Right at Home in China," *Miami Herald*, July 13, 2002.

Robert Dreyfuss — "Big Tobacco Rides East," *Mother Jones*, January/February 1999. www.mojones.com.

Debra Efroymson and Saifuddin Ahmed — "Hungry for Tobacco, an Analysis of the Economic Impact of Tobacco on the Poor in Bangladesh," PATH Canada, October 2001. www.pathcanada.org.

Ross Hammond and Andy Rowell — "Trust Us: We're the Tobacco Industry," Action on Smoking and Health (UK), May 2001. www.ash.org.uk.

Richard McCaffery — "Philip Morris on the Hot Seat," The Motley Fool, August 2, 2001. www.fool.com.

J. Prabhat and
F.J. Chaloupka

"Curbing the Epidemic: Governments and the Economics of Tobacco Control," The World Bank, May 1999. www.1.worldbank.org.

Kenneth E. Warner

"Tobacco," *Foreign Policy*, May/June 2002.

World Health
Organization

"Young Women's Smoking Crisis Set to Hit Asia," November 15, 1999. www.who.int.

# For Further Discussion

## Chapter 1

1. The *Medical Letter on the CDC and FDA* discusses research indicating that smoking is a greater health risk than previously believed. Robert A. Levy, however, maintains that the government has exaggerated the harmfulness of smoking. Which viewpoint do you think is more convincing? Why?

2. The Mayo Clinic insists that secondhand smoke causes many health problems, especially in children. Jeffrey Hart argues that there is no scientific basis for attributing illness to exposure to secondhand smoke, and that those who insist that secondhand smoke is harmful are doing so to be politically correct. Each author insists that his argument is based on scientific information. Which argument is stronger? Why?

3. Susan Dominus maintains that teens know the health risks involved in smoking but choose to do it anyway because they consider it "cool." *Cancer Weekly* discusses research showing that smoking is actually decreasing among teenagers, especially young teens who have been strongly influenced by antismoking ads and have little tolerance for smokers. Do you agree that the intolerance young teens have for smoking will keep them from ever starting to use tobacco or will they respond to peer pressure as they get older and try smoking? Cite the viewpoints and draw upon your own experience when constructing your answer.

4. Robert Preidt argues that the use of smokeless or spit tobacco poses a serious health risk. The U.S. Smokeless Tobacco Company (USSTC) contends that smokeless tobacco use is less harmful than cigarette smoking. How does the fact that the USSTC processes and sells smokeless tobacco and Preidt reports on health issues affect the credibility of their respective arguments?

## Chapter 2

1. Christine H. Rowley argues that nicotine is a highly addictive drug, on par with heroin and cocaine. She maintains that the difficulty many people have quitting is proof that they are addicted to the nicotine in tobacco. Dale M. Atrens, however, insists that there is no scientific evidence that nicotine is addictive. He does not regard the fact that many smokers have difficulty quitting as evidence of nicotine addiction. Whose argument best explains the problems people have when they try to stop using tobacco? Explain.

2. Kathiann M. Kowalski insists that despite a 1998 settlement prohibiting tobacco companies from marketing their products to teens, the four major tobacco companies continue to target their advertising to teens so that they will always have a ready supply of new customers. Robert A. Levy claims that the tobacco companies have drastically cut ads in publications aimed at teens and now run ads in general interest publications that teens may or may not read. Whose argument is most believable? Why?

3. Using twin studies similar to those done to determine the genetic basis for alcoholism, scientists have proven that genetic factors play a more important role than environmental factors in determining nicotine addiction, Patrick Zickler contends. What are the implications for those trying to quit smoking if Zickler's theory is accurate? Explain.

## Chapter 3

1. Nicotine is a drug and therefore should be regulated by the Food and Drug Administration (FDA) like any other legal drug, David A. Kessler argues. He contends that federal control of nicotine would make it easier to limit the use of tobacco by teens and children. Michael DeBow insists that the states can do a better job of regulating tobacco than the federal government. He is concerned that the federal government might seek to control tobacco use by adults as well as youths. Which argument is more convincing? Why?

2. Michelle Leverett and her colleagues argue that raising the tax on cigarettes will discourage children and teens from smoking. W. Kip Viscusi insists that poor adults, not children and teens, will feel the greatest impact from the cigarette tax increase. Choose two points from each viewpoint with which you agree and two with which you disagree. Explain your selections.

3. All forms of nicotine replacement therapy (NRT) are effective in helping smokers quit, contend Lisa J. Diefenbach and Patrick O. Smith. Editors from *Formulary*, however, maintain that NRT is not at all effective in helping smokers achieve long-term smoking cessation. Describe the scientific data cited in each viewpoint and explain which authors you think use the data more persuasively.

## Chapter 4

1. Iraj Abedian argues that tobacco use is reaching epidemic proportions in the developing world and within the next thirty years will be the single largest cause of death worldwide. FORCES International, however, claims that global public health agencies

have distorted science to inflate the number of deaths and exaggerate the problem of tobacco use worldwide. Which argument uses scientific data more persuasively? Cite from the viewpoints while constructing your answer.

2. Noy Thrupkaew insists that transnational tobacco companies target women with clever advertising campaigns, which has resulted in increasing numbers of women worldwide becoming addicted to tobacco. Should national governments become more involved in restricting advertising that is aimed at women? Cite from the viewpoint as you explain.

# Organizations to Contact

The editors have compiled the following list of organizations concerned with the issues debated in this book. The descriptions are derived from materials provided by the organizations. All have publications or information available for interested readers. The list was compiled on the date of publication of the present volume; the information provided here may change. Be aware that many organizations take several weeks or longer to respond to inquiries, so allow as much time as possible.

**Action on Smoking and Health (ASH)**
2013 H St. NW, Washington, DC 20006
(202) 659-4310
website: www.ash.org

Action on Smoking and Health promotes the rights of nonsmokers and works to protect them from the harms of smoking. ASH worked to eliminate tobacco ads from radio and television and to ban smoking in airplanes, buses, and many public places. The organization publishes the bimonthly newsletter *ASH Smoking and Health Review* and fact sheets on a variety of topics, including teen smoking, passive smoking, and nicotine addiction.

**Airspace Action on Smoking and Health (ASASH)**
6200 McKay Ave., Box 141-831, Burnaby, BC V5H 4M9 Canada
(888) 621-7233 • (604) 444-8016 • fax: (604) 276-3247
e-mail: airspace@airspace.bc.ca • website: www.airspace.bc.ca

Airspace Action on Smoking and Health seeks to eliminate tobacco smoking. The group lobbies for more stringent laws banning smoking in public places and offers help to those trying to stop smoking.

**American Cancer Society**
1599 Clifton Rd. NE, Atlanta, GA 30329
(800) ACS-2345 (227-2345)
website: www.cancer.org

The American Cancer Society is one of the primary organizations in the United States devoted to educating the public about cancer and to funding cancer research. The society spends a great deal of its resources on educating the public about the dangers of smoking and on lobbying for antismoking legislation. The American Cancer Society makes available hundreds of publications, ranging from reports and surveys to position papers.

**American Council on Science and Health (ACSH)**
1995 Broadway, 2nd Fl., New York, NY 10023-5860
(212) 362-7044 • fax: (212) 362-4919
e-mail: acsh@acsh.org • website: www.acsh.org

ACSH is a consumer education group concerned with issues related to food, nutrition, chemicals, pharmaceuticals, lifestyle, the environment, and health. It publishes the quarterly newsletter *Priorities* as well as the booklets *The Tobacco Industry's Use of Nicotine as a Drug* and *Marketing Cigarettes to Kids.*

**American Lung Association (ALA)**
1740 Broadway, New York, NY 10019-4374
(212) 315-8700 • fax: (212) 265-5642
e-mail: info@lungusa.org • website: www.lungusa.org

Founded in 1904, the American Lung Association is the oldest voluntary health agency in the United States. It is dedicated to the prevention, cure, and control of all types of lung disease, including asthma, emphysema, tuberculosis, and lung cancer. ALA's mission is to prevent lung disease and to promote lung health.

**American Medical Association (AMA)**
515 N. State St., Chicago, IL 60610
(312) 464-5000
website: www.ama-assn.org

The AMA is the largest professional association for medical doctors. It helps set standards for medical education and practices, and is a powerful lobby in Washington for physicians' interests. It publishes the *Journal of the American Medical Association.*

**Americans for Nonsmokers' Rights**
2530 San Pablo Ave., Suite J, Berkeley, CA 94702
(510) 841-3032 • fax: (510) 841-3071
e-mail: anr@no-smoke.org • website: www.no-smoke.org

Americans for Nonsmokers' Rights seeks to protect the rights of nonsmokers in the workplace and other public settings. It works with the American Nonsmokers' Rights Foundation, which promotes smoking prevention, nonsmokers' rights, and public education about involuntary smoking. The organization publishes the quarterly newsletter *ANR Update*, the book *Clearing the Air*, and the guidebook *How to Butt In: Teens Take Action.*

**Canadian Council for Tobacco Control (CCTC)**
75 Albert St., Suite 508, Ottawa, ON K1P 5E7 Canada
(800) 267-5234 • (613) 567-3050 • fax: (613) 567-5695
e-mail: info-services@cctc.ca • website: www.cctc.ca

The CCTC works to ensure a healthier society, free from addiction and involuntary exposure to tobacco products. It promotes a comprehensive tobacco control program involving educational, social, fiscal, and legislative interventions. It publishes several fact sheets, including *Promoting a Lethal Product* and *The Ban on Smoking on School Property: Successes and Challenges.*

**Cato Institute**
1000 Massachusetts Ave. NW, Washington, DC 20001
(202) 842-0200
website: www.cato.org

The institute is a libertarian public policy research foundation dedicated to limiting the control of government and protecting individual liberty. Its quarterly magazine *Regulation* has published articles and letters questioning the accuracy of EPA studies on the dangers of secondhand smoke. The *Cato Journal* is published by the institute three times a year and the *Cato Policy Analysis* occasional papers are published periodically.

**Children Opposed to Smoking Tobacco (COST)**
Mary Volz School, 509 W. 3rd Ave., Runnemede, NJ 08078
e-mail: costkids@costkids.org
website: www.costkids.org

COST was founded in 1996 by a group of middle school students committed to keeping tobacco products out of the hands of children. Much of the organization's efforts are spent fighting the tobacco industry's advertising campaigns directed at children and teenagers. Articles, such as "Environmental Tobacco Smoke," "What Is a Parent To Do?," and "What You Can Do," are available on its website.

**Coalition on Smoking OR Health**
1150 Connecticut Ave. NW, Suite 820, Washington, DC 20036
(202) 452-1184

Formed by the American Lung Association, the American Heart Association, and the American Cancer Society, the coalition has worked to revise warning labels on tobacco products and to ban smoking in public places. It seeks to restrict advertising of tobacco products, to increase tobacco taxes, to regulate tobacco products, and to prohibit youths' access to tobacco products. It publishes the report *Tobacco Use: An American Crisis*, the briefing kits Leveling the Playing Field and Saving Lives and Raising Revenue, as well as fact sheets and several annual publications.

**Environmental Protection Agency (EPA)**
Indoor Air Quality Information Clearinghouse
PO Box 37133, Washington, DC 20013-7133
(800) 438-4318 • (703) 356-4020 • fax: (703) 356-5386
e-mail: iaqinfo@aol.com • website: www.epa.gov
The EPA is the agency of the U.S. government that coordinates actions designed to protect the environment. It promotes indoor air quality standards that reduce the dangers of secondhand smoke. The EPA publishes and distributes reports such as *Respiratory Health Effects of Passive Smoking: Lung Cancer and Other Disorders* and *What You Can Do About Secondhand Smoke as Parents, Decision-makers, and Building Occupants.*

**Fight Ordinances & Restrictions to Control & Eliminate Smoking (FORCES)**
PO Box 14347, San Francisco, CA 94114-0347
(415) 675-0157
e-mail: info@forces.org • website: www.forces.org
FORCES fights against smoking ordinances and restrictions designed to eventually eliminate smoking, and it works to increase public awareness of smoking-related legislation. It opposes any state or local ordinance it feels is not fair to those who choose to smoke. Although FORCES does not advocate smoking, it asserts that an individual has the right to choose to smoke and that smokers should be accommodated where and when possible. FORCES publishes *Tobacco Weekly* as well as many articles.

**Food and Drug Administration (FDA)**
5600 Fishers Ln., Rockville, MD 20857
(888) INFO-FDA (888-463-6332)
website: www.fda.gov
An agency of the U.S. government charged with protecting the health of the public against impure and unsafe foods, drugs, cosmetics, and other potential hazards, the FDA has sought the regulation of nicotine as a drug and has investigated manipulation of nicotine levels in cigarettes by the tobacco industry. It provides copies of congressional testimony given in the debate over regulation of nicotine.

**Foundation for Economic Education**
30 S. Broadway, Irvington-on-Hudson, NY 10533
(914) 591-7230 • fax: (914) 591-8910
e-mail: fee@fee.org • website: www.fee.org
The foundation promotes private property rights, the free market economic system, and limited government. Its monthly journal, the *Freeman*, has published articles opposing regulation of the tobacco industry.

**Group Against Smoking Pollution (GASP)**
PO Box 632, College Park, MD 20741-0632
(301) 459-4791
Consisting of nonsmokers adversely affected by tobacco smoke, GASP works to promote the rights of nonsmokers, to educate the public about the problems of secondhand smoke, and to encourage the regulation of smoking in public places. The organization provides information and referral services and distributes educational materials, buttons, posters, and bumper stickers. GASP publishes booklets and pamphlets such as *The Nonsmokers' Bill of Rights* and *The Nonsmokers' Liberation Guide*.

**International Network of Women Against Tobacco (INWAT)**
c/o Bonnie Kantor, PO Box 224, Metuchen, NJ 08840
(732) 549-9054 • fax: (732) 549-9056
e-mail: bonnie@inwat.org • website: www.inwat.org
The International Network of Women Against Tobacco provides contacts and information to individuals, particularly women, working for tobacco control. The group disseminates information about global tobacco issues, helps develop strategies to counter tobacco advertising, and supports the development of women-centered tobacco cessation programs. They publish fact sheets about tobacco issues and a quarterly newsletter.

**KidsHealth.org**
The Nemours Foundation Center for Children's Health Media
1600 Rockland Rd., Wilmington, DE 19803
(302) 651-4000 • fax: (302) 651-4077
e-mail: info@KidsHealth.org • website: www.KidsHealth.org
The mission of KidsHealth.org is to help families make informed decisions about children's health by creating the highest quality health media. It utilizes cutting-edge technology and a wealth of trusted medical resources to provide the best in pediatric health information. Its teen section covers a wide variety of issues, in-

cluding teen smoking. *How to Raise Non-Smoking Kids* and *Smoking: Cutting Through the Hype* are two of its numerous publications.

**Libertarian Party**
1528 Pennsylvania Ave. SE, Washington, DC 20003
website: www.lp.org
The goal of this political party is to ensure respect for individual rights. It opposes regulation of smoking. The party publishes the bimonthly *Libertarian Party News* and periodic *Issue Papers*.

**National Center for Tobacco-Free Kids/Campaign for Tobacco-Free Kids**
1707 L St. NW, Suite 800, Washington, DC 20036
(800) 284-KIDS (284-5437)
e-mail: info@tobaccofreekids.org
website: www.tobaccofreekids.org
The National Center for Tobacco-Free Kids/Campaign for Tobacco-Free Kids is the largest private initiative ever launched to protect children from tobacco addiction. The center works in partnership with the American Cancer Society and over one hundred other health, civic, corporate, youth, and religious organizations. Among the center's publications are press releases, reports, and fact sheets, including *Tobacco Use Among Youth*, *Tobacco Marketing to Kids*, and *Smokeless (Spit) Tobacco and Kids*.

**Reason Foundation**
3415 S. Sepulveda Blvd., Suite 400, Los Angeles, CA 90034
(310) 391-2245
website: www.reason.org
The Reason Foundation is a libertarian research and education foundation that works to promote free markets and limited government. It publishes the monthly *Reason* magazine, which occasionally contains articles opposing the regulation of smoking.

**SmokeFree Educational Services, Inc.**
375 South End Ave., Suite 32F, New York, NY 10280
(212) 912-0960
website: www.smokefreeair.org
This organization works to educate youth on the relationship between smoking and health. It publishes the quarterly newsletter *SmokeFree Air* and the book *Kids Say Don't Smoke* and distributes posters, stickers, and videotapes.

**Society for Research on Nicotine and Tobacco**
7600 Terrace Ave., Suite 203, Middleton, WI 53562
(608) 836-3787 • (608) 831-5485
e-mail: srnt@tmahq.com • website: www.srnt.org
The Society for Research on Nicotine and Tobacco fosters the exchange of information on the entire spectrum of research concerning tobacco use and nicotine dependence. The group publishes a monthly newsletter and a bimonthly journal, *Nicotine and Tobacco Research*.

**The Tobacco Institute**
1875 I St., NW, Washington, DC 20006
website: www.tobaccoinstitute.com
The institute is the primary national lobbying organization for the tobacco industry. The institute argues that the dangers of smoking have not been proven and opposes regulation of tobacco. It provides the public with general information on smoking issues.

**Tobacco Merchants Association of the United States**
PO Box 8019, Princeton, NJ 08543-8019
(609) 275-4900 • fax: (609) 275-8379
e-mail: tma@tma.org • website: www.tma.org
The association represents manufacturers of tobacco products; tobacco leaf dealers, suppliers, and distributors; and others related to the tobacco industry. It tracks statistics on the sale and distribution of tobacco and informs its members of this information through the following periodicals: the weekly newsletters *Executive Summary*, *World Alert*, and *Tobacco Weekly*; the biweekly *Leaf Bulletin and Legislative Bulletin*; the monthly *Trademark Report* and *Tobacco Barometer: Smoking, Chewing & Snuff*; and the quarterly newsletter *Issues Monitor*. The association has a reference library, offers online services, and provides economic, statistical, media-tracking, legislative, and regulatory information.

**Tobacco Products Liability Project (TPLP)**
Tobacco Control Resource Center
Northeastern University School of Law
400 Huntington Ave., Boston, MA 02115-5098
(617) 373-2026 • fax: (617) 373-3672
e-mail: tobacco@bigfoot.com
Founded in 1984 by doctors, academics, and attorneys, TPLP studies, encourages, and coordinates product liability suits in order to publicize the effects of smoking on health. It publishes the monthly newsletter *Tobacco on Trial*.

# Bibliography of Books

Harold V. Cordry — *Tobacco: A Reference Handbook.* Santa Barbara, CA: ABC-CLIO, 2001.

John Crofton and David Simpson — *Tobacco: A Global Threat.* New York: Macmillan Education, 2002.

Joy De Boyer et al., eds. — *Tobacco Control Policies: Strategies, Successes, and Setbacks.* Washington, DC: World Bank, 2003.

Hanan Frenk and Reuven Dar — *A Critique of Nicotine Addiction.* Cambridge, MA: Kluwer Academic, 2000.

Stanton A. Glantz and Edith D. Balbach — *The Tobacco War: Inside the California Battles.* Berkeley: University of California Press, 2000.

Stanton A. Glantz et al. — *The Cigarette Papers.* Berkeley: University of California Press, 1998.

Michael G. Goldstein et al. — *The Tobacco Dependence Treatment Handbook: A Guide to Best Practices.* New York: Guilford Press, 2003.

Lorraine Greaves — *Smoke Screen: Women's Smoking and Social Control.* London: Scarlet Press, 1999.

John Harvey and M.D. Kellogg — *Tobaccoism or How Tobacco Kills.* Kita, MT: Kessinger, 2003.

Jason Hughes — *Learning to Smoke: Tobacco Use in the West.* Chicago: University of Chicago Press, 2003.

Leonard A. Jason et al., eds. — *Preventing Youth Access to Tobacco.* Binghamton, NY: Haworth Press, 2003.

Prabhat Jha and Frank J. Chaloupka, eds. — *Tobacco Control in Developing Countries.* New York: Oxford University Press, 2000.

David Kessler — *A Question of Intent: A Great American Battle with a Deadly Industry.* New York: Public Affairs, 2002.

Lynn T. Kozlowski et al. — *Cigarettes, Nicotine, and Health.* Thousand Oaks, CA: Sage, 2001.

Mike A. Males — *Smoked: Why Joe Camel Is Still Smiling.* Monroe, ME: Common Courage Press, 1999.

Carrick Mollenkamp et al. — *The People vs. Big Tobacco: How the States Took on the Cigarette Giants.* New York: Bloomberg Press, 1998.

Laury Oaks — *Smoking and Pregnancy: The Politics of Fetal Protection.* Piscataway, NJ: Rutgers University Press, 2001.

Tara Parker-Pope — *Cigarettes: Anatomy of an Industry from Seed to Smoke.* New York: New Press, 2001.

| Michael Pertschuk | *Smoke in Their Eyes: Lessons in Movement Leadership from the Tobacco Wars.* Nashville, TN: Vanderbilt University Press, 2001. |

Robert L Rabin and Stephen D. Sugarman, eds.  
*Regulating Tobacco.* New York: Oxford University Press, 2001.

Pamela Rogers and Steve Baldwin  
*Controlled or Reduced Smoking.* Westport, CT: Greenwood Press, 1999.

Kathleen Stratton et al., eds.  
*Clearing the Smoke: Assessing the Science Base for Tobacco Harm Reduction.* Washington, DC: National Academy Press, 2001.

Donley T. Studlar  
*Tobacco Control: Comparative Politics in the United States and Canada.* Orchard Park, NY: Broadview Press, 2002.

Ian Tyrrell  
*Deadly Enemies: Tobacco and Its Opponents in Australia.* New South Wales, Australia: New South Wales University Press, 2000.

W. Kip Viscusi  
*Smoke-Filled Rooms: A Postmortem on the Tobacco Deal.* Chicago: University of Chicago Press, 2002.

Ronald R. Watson and Mark L. Witten, eds.  
*Environmental Tobacco Smoke.* Boca Raton, FL: CRC Press, 2000.

C. J. Westfield  
*The Cost of Using Tobacco.* Bloomington, IN: 1st Books Library, 2002.

Adam Winters and Michael Sommers  
*Tobacco and Your Mouth: The Incredibly Disgusting Story.* New York: Rosen, 2000.

Mark Wolfson  
*The Fight Against Big Tobacco: The Movement, the State, and the Public's Health.* Berlin: Aldine de Gruyter, 2001.

# Index